IN THE S'l ... S
OF JANE AUSTEN

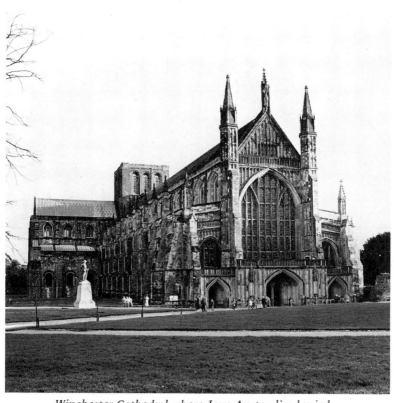

Winchester Cathedral where Jane Austen lies buried

In the Steps of
JANE AUSTEN

ANNE-MARIE EDWARDS

Photographs by Michael Edwards

J O N E S
B O O K S
Madison, Wisconsin

Jones Books
309 N. Hillside Terrace
Madison, Wisconsin 53705-3328
www.jonesbooks.com

This edition was published by arrangement with
Countryside Books, Newbury, Berkshire, England.

First North American edition 2003

ISBN 0-9721217-0-6

Maps drawn by Julie Edwards, based on Ordnance Survey
Maps with the permission of the Controller of Her Majesty's
Stationery Office, England. Crown Copyright reserved.

Library of Congress Control Number: 2002115568

Printed in the United States of America

Contents

List of Illustrations

Acknowledgements

I would like to thank all those I have met on my travels who have helped me to make this book: Mr Richards, Mr Burrell and the staff of Southampton Library, the staff of Totton Library, the staff of the West Country Studies Library in Exeter, and the curators and staff of the Lyme Regis Museum and the Winchester City Museum. Rev. Turner, Rev. W. B. Norris and Mr G. Mann gave me valuable information about Steventon; Mrs E. Hogg, Rev. Gardner and Mr Steward assisted me with the Ibthorpe chapter; Mr Montgomery gave me information about Goodnestone and Mr Berrett guided me at Godmersham. Mrs M. E. Coleman helped me with my research. In London I was assisted on my first visit by Mr Stimpson and the staff of the Greater London Council Covent Garden Team and recently by Mr Chris Curry of Acorn Computers and John and Bev Murphy. We were also assisted by Mr Clifford S. Sympson of Goodwin's Court. I received more information about Lyme Regis from Mr Batten and information about Deane Gate from Peter Fuller. I am very grateful to Alec and Sue O'Connor, the Dowager Countess of Iddesleigh, Ms Pam Stephens, Mr and Mrs Russell Cornall and Mrs E. M. Cornall for valuable help with the Devon chapter. My thanks to Mrs Anne Mallinson for help and encouragement, to Mr Tim Neale at Radio Solent for his support and to my friends at Countryside Books, Nicholas and Suzanne Battle, for their advice on editorial and production. For the friendly welcome and help I have always received at Chawton Cottage I would like to thank Mrs Rose, Mr and Mrs John Coates and Miss Jean Bowden. Miss Bowden helped with notes for the 3rd edition, and gave me valuable suggestions for this new edition. For help in checking routes for this edition I am most grateful to Anne and Denis Thompson.

Pictures of the interior of Chawton Cottage were taken by permission of Mr John Coates on behalf of the Jane Austen Memorial Trust; of the interior of 10 Henrietta Street by permission of Mr Chris Curry; of Chawton House by permission of Mrs Knight; of Deane House by permission of Oliver and Veronica Baring; of Ashe House by permission of the proprietor; and of Ibthorpe House by permission of Mrs E. Hogg. The print of Northam Bridge is reproduced by courtesy of Southampton Library, the print of Godmersham House by courtesy of Kent County Library and the print of the Pump Room, Bath by courtesy of the Victoria Art Gallery, Bath City Council. The engraving of a group of waltzers, from *La Belle Assemblée*, 1 February 1817, is reproduced by courtesy of the Trustees of the Victoria and Albert Museum.

It is a pleasure to be able to thank Beth Young for her editorial advice, Pauline Newton for her patient typesetting and Louise Burston for designing the book and helping at every stage of its production.

I am grateful to all my friends for their encouragement, especially Mary, whose cheerful support never fails. And finally, I thank my family – my daughter Julie who drew the maps with such care, my son Chris who checked all the routes with seamanlike precision and my husband Mike, who while still performing miracles with map and compass managed to take the photographs as well!

Quotations from *Jane Austen's Letters*, ed. R. W. Chapman, are made by kind permission of the Oxford University Press (spelling has been modernised). The maps are based on Ordnance Survey maps.

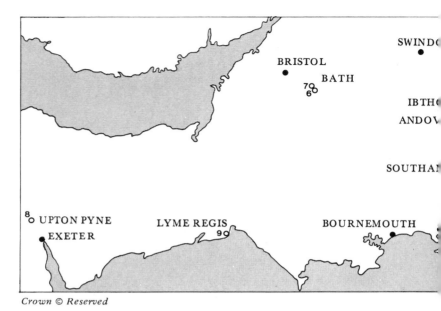

SWIND(

BRISTOL

BATH

7○
6○

IBTH(

ANDOV

SOUTHAI

8
○ UPTON PYNE   LYME REGIS   BOURNEMOUTH

●EXETER   9○

All the routes have been carefully checked, before going to press, with the appropriate County Definitive Maps, and follow public rights of way or paths to which the public have been granted access by the landowner. However, these are vulnerable to change and the publisher and the copyright owner accept no responsibility for any consequences arising out of use of this book, including misinterpretation of the maps and directions. It is sometimes difficult to distinguish a right of way across farmland. Supplement these directions with a good map — not less than 1 inch to the mile — and you should experience few problems. To protect our good name and the livelihood of the farmer, ensure that grazing animals are not disturbed, guard against fire and fasten all gates.

Introduction

Jane Austen has sometimes been depicted as a rather prim spinster, living a restricted life within the confines of a country village. Nothing could be further from the truth. She was a Georgian woman, with an open, critical mind and a robust eighteenth-century attitude towards life. She had no illusions about human nature, she was accustomed to the sight of poverty and death. As the parson's daughter she helped her father care for the poor in his parish, and at Chawton she was concerned with the folk on her brother Edward's estate. Neither was she sheltered from the harsh realities of the great events of the time: a favourite cousin's husband was guillotined in the French revolution and her two sailor brothers were on active service throughout the major battles of the Napoleonic wars. But although the effects of the long war are apparent in Jane's novels, she is concerned to write about life within her own direct experience. She knew that important as external events may be, society is built around the family and marriage is the knot that holds the family together. Making the right choice of partner is all-important. This involved all the social activities which characterised her world: calling on newcomers, visiting friends and acquaintances at regular intervals, dinners and dances at small country houses as well as grander occasions held at inns, or the local Assembly Rooms. In those days of home entertainment, an accomplished woman needed to be a good conversationalist and a musician, as well as an efficient housekeeper. Jane gives us the whole picture in her novels.

Although Jane was always proud of being 'a Hampshire-born Austen', her world was by no means confined to Steventon, the small village near Basingstoke where she was born, or Chawton where she spent the last years of her life. She visited Kent frequently, spent much time in Bath and knew London well. She stayed with relatives at Great Bookham, near Box Hill in Surrey, and spent summers by the sea in several resorts including Lyme Regis which she recalls with so much delight in *Persuasion*. The Austens were not rich and Jane usually walked to visit friends and to shop. She walked too for pleasure, believing lovely scenery to be 'one of the joys of heaven'.

Today we can walk in Jane's footsteps and still capture a great deal of the atmosphere of her world. The country houses, churches, great estates and elegant cities she knew have changed surprisingly little in the course of two centuries. I have found exploring Jane's England a most rewarding experience. I hope you will too.

Calendar

1760 Accession of George III — **1762** Rousseau *Social Contract* — **1764** Horace Walpole *The Castle of Otranto: a romantic novel*. Foundation of 'The Club' which included Boswell, Burke, Garrick, Goldsmith, Johnson and Reynolds — **1765** Robert Adam designed Lansdowne House. Launching of HMS *Victory* — **1776** Adam Smith *The Wealth of Nations* — **1778** Fanny Burney *Evelina* — **1780** Johnson *Lives of the Poets* — **1789** French Revolution began (Jane's cousin, Eliza, escaped but Eliza's husband, the Comte de Feuillide, was executed) — **1788** Haydn *Oxford Symphony in G*. Mozart *Jupiter Symphony* — **1790** Repton summarised the new 'natural' principles applied to landscape gardening which Lancelot 'Capability' Brown had been applying to English estates since the mid-century (discussed by Jane's characters) — **1791** Tom Paine *Rights of Man* — **1792** Outbreak of the Napoleonic Wars (the effect of these long wars is in the background of Jane's later work). Gilpin published essays on 'the picturesque' in art and landscape (much discussed by Jane's characters) — **1798** Wordsworth and Coleridge *The Lyrical Ballads* (the *Preface* was the manifesto of the Romantic movement) — **1805** Battle of Trafalgar (Jane's brother Frank was serving in Nelson's fleet but missed this battle) — **1809** Defeat at Corunna (Frank was in charge of the disembarkation of Sir John Moore's troops) — **1811** Prince of Wales became Regent (Jane was requested to dedicate *Emma* to him) — 1815 Napoleon escaped from Elba (Jane's brothers, Frank and Charles, were on duty in the Mediterranean). Battle of Waterloo — 1818 Byron *Childe Harold*.

1775– 1787	On 16 December 1775, Jane Austen was born at Steventon Rectory, in North Hampshire. She was the seventh of eight children. They were a happy, loving family. Jane and her sister Cassandra were devoted to each other. When Jane was six her lively cousin Eliza married the Comte de Feuillide and visited Steventon. Private theatricals took place in the barn at Steventon. Before she was eleven Jane had accompanied Cassandra to school in Oxford, Southampton and Reading. After the age of eleven she was educated at home, probably being tutored by her father, an ex-fellow of St John's College. He possessed a good library and she read widely.
1787– 1792	From around the age of twelve Jane was constantly writing sketches and stories which she gathered into *Volume the First, Volume the Second* and *Volume the Third*. These included *Love and Friendship*, a burlesque of over-sentimental fiction, and her very personal *History of England*.
1792	A visit in September, to former Steventon friends Martha and Mary Lloyd, at Ibthorpe near Hurstbourne Tarrant, probably helped Jane characterise Lady Susan in her story of that name.
1793	Jane's brother Frank (a year older than Jane), now a lieutenant, came home on leave. Possibly Jane danced with him in Southampton. Her pride in her sailor brother is recalled by that of Fanny in her brother William in *Mansfield Park*.
1794	Eliza's husband was guillotined in France. During a visit to the Leigh Perrots in Bath Jane enjoyed the balls and all the social activities that she pictured in *Susan* (later re-titled *Northanger Abbey*).

1795   Jane probably wrote *Susan* before working on *Elinor and Marianne* (which she was to revise extensively before its publication as *Sense and Sensibility*).

1796   In January Jane described in letters to Cassandra some of the parties and dances she enjoyed in the homes of their friends, particularly at Ashe House where she flirted with Tom Lefroy. Breaking her journey in London, Jane visited her brother Edward and his wife Elizabeth, in Kent. While she stayed with them at Rowling near Goodnestone, she gathered ideas for her next novel, *First Impressions*.

1797   By the end of the year she had completed *First Impressions* (to be revised later and published as *Pride and Prejudice*). Her father offered it to Cadell in November who refused it. In the same month Jane and Cassandra visited Bath with Mrs Austen. Jane's favourite brother Henry married Eliza.

1798   Jane visited Edward in Kent at Godmersham, the large estate he had inherited from their relatives, the Knights, who had adopted him as a boy. She gathered hints for the character of Darcy (*Pride and Prejudice*) and Miss Bates and Mrs Elton (*Emma*).

1799   It is likely that Jane visited the Cookes at Great Bookham as she used a Surrey setting for *The Watsons* and *Emma*. Jane accompanied Edward to Bath and enjoyed country walks as well as firework displays and visits to the theatre. She returned home in June.

1800   Jane accompanied Martha Lloyd to Ibthorpe at the end of the year. When she returned to Steventon Mrs Austen told her they had decided to retire to Bath.

1801   Early in the year the Austens moved to Bath. They stayed with the Leigh Perrots and spent a summer holiday in Sidmouth. They returned to Bath in the autumn to move into their new house, 4 Sydney Terrace.

1802   Jane spent a summer holiday in Dawlish and Teignmouth. Possibly at this time she experienced a serious love affair. The young man died within a few weeks of their meeting. In November Jane and Cassandra stayed with James at Steventon and visited the Bigg Withers at Manydown. Harris Bigg Wither proposed to Jane and she accepted him. In the morning she changed her mind.

1803   Jane possibly stayed for a while at Godmersham as she visited Frank at Ramsgate. She made a final revision of *Susan* which she sold to Crosby for £10.

1804   Late in the year the Austens took a short holiday in Lyme Regis. Jane recalled her memories of Lyme in *Persuasion*. The family returned to 27 Green Park Buildings, Bath. Here she possibly began *The Watsons* which she never finished.

1805   Jane's father died and the Austens moved to 25 Gay Street. Mrs Lloyd died in April and Martha Lloyd joined them. Cassandra and Jane visited Godmersham and Goodnestone.

1806   The Austens left Bath in July to stay with Frank — newly married to Mary Gibson — in lodgings in Southampton.

1807   They moved into a house in Castle Square, Southampton. In September Jane visited Chawton House, part of Edward's inheritance.

1808   On her way to Godmersham Jane stayed with Henry in Brompton. She returned to Southampton in July and heard in October of the death of Edward's wife, Elizabeth. Edward offered the Austen ladies a home at Godmersham or Chawton. They chose Chawton Cottage.

1809   Jane possibly visited Frank at Portsmouth in March. The Austens left Southampton in April (possibly visited Great Bookham and Godmersham) and arrived in Chawton in July.

1810   Jane worked on the final version of *Sense and Sensibility* to be published at her own expense by T. Egerton of Whitehall.

1811   Jane began *Mansfield Park*. In April she stayed in London with Henry and Eliza and corrected the proofs of *Sense and Sensibility*. She returned to Chawton in May. In November *Sense and Sensibility* was published.

1812   Jane interrupted *Mansfield Park* to revise *First Impressions*, now called *Pride and Prejudice*. She sold it to her publisher for £110. Edward stayed at Chawton House with his eldest daughter Fanny.

1813   *Pride and Prejudice* was published in January. Jane continued writing *Mansfield Park*. After the death of his wife Eliza in April, Henry visited Chawton and drove Jane back to London for a short stay. Edward and his family spent much of their time at Chawton House. Jane finished *Mansfield Park* 'soon after June'. In September she accompanied Edward back to Godmersham, breaking the journey to stay with Henry in Henrietta Street. The second edition of *Sense and Sensibility* was published.

1814   In January Jane began *Emma*. In March she visited Henry in London. *Mansfield Park* was published by Egerton in May and the edition had sold out by the autumn. In June, Jane stayed with the Cookes at Great Bookham and possibly visited Box Hill, the scene of the picnic in *Emma*. Later in the year she visited Henry at Hans Place.

1815   Jane finished *Emma* at the end of March. She began writing *Persuasion* in August. She visited Henry and nursed him through a severe illness. Henry had arranged for Murrays to publish the second edition of *Mansfield Park* and *Emma* which was published in December.

1816   Jane was not well but she continued working on

Persuasion. In May she visited Cheltenham with Cassandra. Jane finished *Persuasion* in July but she was dissatisfied with the ending and rewrote the climax.

1817   Early in the year Jane began a new novel, *Sanditon*. *Susan* — which she had bought back from Crosby for £10 — was 'put on the shelve for the present'. Jane's health began failing rapidly. She travelled with Cassandra to Winchester taking lodgings in College Street but little could be done. Jane died on 18 July and was buried in Winchester Cathedral.

Northanger Abbey (originally *Susan*) and *Persuasion* were published in 1818.

1

Steventon — Home and Family

'Last night the time came, and without a great deal of warning, everything was soon happily over. We have now another girl, a present plaything for her sister Cassy and a future companion. She is to be Jenny . . .' So wrote the Reverend George Austen, rector of the north Hampshire village of Steventon, to his sister-in-law Mrs Walter, announcing the birth of his second daughter. His 'Jenny' was to become one of England's greatest novelists.

Born on 16 December 1775, Jane was the Austens' seventh child. Their eldest son, James, was ten. George, born the following year, suffered from fits and never lived at home. Then came Edward, the sensible, practical son, who was to be adopted by rich relatives and inherit large estates. Henry, born in 1771, handsome and witty, was considered by his father the most brilliant of his sons. He was Jane's favourite brother. Her sister Cassandra, to whom she was devoted, was born in 1773, and another brother, Frank, arrived the following year. After Jane, another son, Charles, was born in 1779. Jane called him 'our own particular little brother'. Frank and Charles entered the Royal Navy and both rose to the rank of Admiral. As she grew up within the circle of this loving and talented family, Jane was able to develop the personal qualities which give her books their moral integrity and improve and polish her own natural gifts as a writer.

She spent the first twenty-five years of her life in Steventon. From an early age she was constantly writing, mostly comic pieces, to amuse her family. Like Walter Scott, she delighted in what his biographer calls 'the queerness and the fun'. Among these early works, which she collected into Volume the first, Volume the second, and Volume the third, each solemnly dedicated to appropriate members of her family and her friends, is a clever burlesque of an over-sentimental romantic novel, called *Love and Friendship*. At one point the rigours endured by the two heroes, the harsh attitudes of parents and the influence of their own emotions provoke this delicious parody of excessive romanticism: 'It was too pathetic for the feelings of Sophia and myself — we fainted alternately on the sofa!' Jane also includes an amusing History of England which she describes as being by 'a partial, prejudic'd and ignorant historian'. By the time she was twenty Jane was writing *First Impressions* which she was to 'lop and crop' and later publish as *Pride and Prejudice*. The original versions of *Sense and Sensibility* and *Northanger Abbey* were also written at Steventon.

As Jane based her art on truthful and accurate observation of the life around her, she could, as she remarked, find plenty to write about in a small country village. And life in the rectory was never dull. Her mother, noted for her humour, passed this gift on to her children. She termed it their 'sprack wit'. Jane sharpened this humour, based on good sense, into a brilliant weapon with which she fought sham of every kind. Her father, an ex-fellow of St John's College, was a fine scholar. He prepared James and Henry for Oxford and Jane shared in their reading. Among her favourite writers Jane included Johnson, Cowper, Goldsmith, Fielding and Richardson but she also delighted in the latest romances of Fanny Burney and the 'Gothic' horror tales of Mrs Radcliffe. She parodies some of these tales of lurid adventure, especially the hair-raising *Mysteries of Udolpho*, in *Northanger Abbey*. In Jane's story, the beautiful and accomplished heroine of the Gothic novel becomes the rather ordinary Catherine Morland, delighted to overhear her parents comment: 'Catherine grows quite a good-looking girl; she is almost pretty today.' Catherine is humiliated to discover that her grave suspicions, fostered by her reading of melodramatic romances, about General Tilney's treatment of his wife at the Abbey, are groundless. But later, when the General exposes Catherine to the dangers of a long journey home, unaccompanied, and as far as he knows, penniless, Jane makes the point that real life can contain happenings as painful as any in Mrs Radcliffe's farfetched dramas. Family discussions must often have found their way into Jane's novels as her characters talk about matters of the moment like the cult of the 'picturesque' in art and nature and the passion for landscape gardening as country gentlemen pursued the new natural look for their estates under the guidance of Repton and Capability Brown.

Through her family, Jane was kept in touch with the great events of her time. One of their cousins, the enchanting and sophisticated Eliza, born in India and educated in France, visited Steventon. She returned to them with the shocking news that her husband had been guillotined in the French Revolution. In her letters, Jane expresses her concern for Sir John Moore's troops at Corunna; she had a first-hand account from Frank who was in charge of their disembarkation in 1809. The effect of the long Napoleonic wars on the civilian population lies behind most of her work. Naughty Lydia Bennet might have behaved better if she had not been dazzled by Wickham's red coat – the effect of billeting the militia on Meryton. Jane also mentions in her letters her care for the poor of her father's parish. "I have given a pair of worsted stockings to Mary Hutchins ... a shift to Hannah Staples and a shawl to Betty Dawkins' and she would be aware of the appalling poverty and squalor that formed so marked a contrast with the elegance and refinement of her time. But the age of fully-fledged romanticism was yet to come. Jane chose to portray the world she knew best; the comfortable, middle-class society of southern England.

Our first walk takes us to Steventon. We ramble in her footsteps along the paths and lanes close to the rectory and through the gentle, rolling countryside she presented so firmly in her novels. The rectory was pulled down soon after her death, but the twelfth-century church where she worshipped stands almost unchanged at the end of a nearby lane. This walk, about seven miles round, begins from the church where there is room to park.

Steventon is about six miles west of Basingstoke. A pleasant approach to the village is through Whitchurch, Laverstoke and Overton, following the B3400 along the Test valley. About two-and-a-half miles from Overton, turn right for Steventon. Drive under the railway and at the junction opposite the village hall, turn left. The road leads past the site of the rectory. Turn right following the sign to the church and park at the end of the lane. Approaching Steventon from the south, from the A30 or M3, take the turn for North Waltham, then follow the lanes for about two miles to Steventon church.

From the church, walk back down the lane to see the site of the rectory. In the eighteenth century this was a rutted cart track which, in bad weather, Jane and Cassandra had to negotiate in their pattens: clog-like overshoes, raised several inches above the ground with iron rings beneath their wooden soles. But in fine weather they walked through the trees beside the road along a path they called 'the Church Walk' which led from their garden. As you approach the corner of the lane, you will see a raised terrace across the field on your left. This was the Austens' 'Wood Walk' which ran west, forming the southern boundary of the home meadows, part of the glebe, or farm land, which belonged to the rectory. The Austens were keenly interested in the efficient running of their farm — Mrs Austen was proud of her dairy and the family had their own recipes for such delights as mead and currant wine — and like most of their contemporaries took pleasure in the laying-out and planting of their garden. Jane writes to Cassandra: 'Our improvements have advanced very well: the bank along the elm walk is sloped down for the reception of thorns and lilacs; and it is settled that the other

Countryside near Steventon

Steventon Church

side of the path is to continue turf'd and planted with beech, ash and larch.' Perhaps she recalls her own childhood pleasures when she tells us that Catherine Morland 'loved nothing so well in the world as rolling down the green slope at the back of the house'.

The rectory stood on the corner, facing north. It was a well-built, two-storied house, with dormer attic windows. Look across the field on the left, about half-way between the terrace and the road, and you will see some railings which enclose an iron pump. This replaced the wooden one which served the Austen household. From the road, a short carriage drive ran to the trellised porch. The front door opened straight into the family parlour where Mrs Austen sat, making shirts and cravats and getting on with the mending in front of visitors, much to the embarrassment of Jane and Cassandra. The two girls shared a small bedroom and sitting room on the first floor, simply furnished with a chocolate-coloured carpet,

The iron pump on the site of the wooden one which served Steventon Rectory. Beyond it is the raised terrace which formed the Austen s' 'Wood Walk'

a press with bookshelves above it, Jane's piano and writing desk with a sloping lid, Cassandra's drawing materials and an oval mirror. Jane's father had a bow-windowed study at the back, overlooking the garden, where he could sit surrounded by his library of over five hundred books. At St John's he had been known as 'the handsome Proctor' and Jane inherited his good looks. In his *Memoir*, her nephew Edward describes her as 'very attractive; her figure was rather tall and slender ... a clear brunette with a rich colour; she had full round cheeks, with mouth and nose small and well-formed, bright, hazel eyes, and brown hair forming natural curls round her face'.

Edward also comments on the happy atmosphere of their home. 'Above all there was strong family affection.' Jane mirrors this love of her family – particularly of her sister – in all her novels. In *Sense and Sensibility*, however foolish the over-sentimental Marianne may be, she never wavers in her devotion to her sister Elinor. Although Jane insists that the best marriages are based on mutual love and esteem – a startingly modern view for her time – parental authority must always be respected. General Tilney must give his blessing to the wedding of his son before the ceremony can take place.

In the field opposite the house stood a large barn where the Austens acted plays. Walk back up the lane to the church. An enormous yew stands sentinel beside this simple building with its slim Early English windows. When Jane's father, rector here for forty years, retired to Bath, James took over the living. You will see memorials to James, and his first wife Anne, in the chancel. The parish register records the marriage of a cousin of the Austens, Jane Cooper, and also some of our Jane's earliest work. THE BANNS OF MARRIAGE BETWEEN (then in her own hand) Henry Frederic Howard Fitzwilliam of London AND Jane Austen of Steventon WERE DULY PUB-LISHED IN THIS CHURCH. Her father's reactions have not been recorded!

Opposite the church a new manor has been built on the

site of a Victorian mansion, all that survived a disastrous fire. Jane knew well the elegant Elizabethan manor which stood nearby until 1970. The tenant-farmers were their friends, the Digweeds.

From the church, turn right along the lane for a few yards. Then follow the footpath sign pointing right over the fields at the side of the church. Make your way towards the corner of the churchyard railings. Then bear half right over the field towards a pine wood and before the wood cross a stile on your right. A ruined brick building is about eighty yards away over the grass on your right. Keep straight ahead with the wood on your left to cross another stile. Turn left to walk beside open fields. The fields slope down to a shallow valley, and a little to the right, rising above the dip, is the squat tower of North Waltham church. Walk along the edge of the field, beside a belt of trees, and follow the fence round as it turns right. After about 100 yards, cross a stile on your left and walk down the field with the church now almost directly ahead. Cross another stile in the valley and walk up the green, with a tall hedge on your left, to a minor road. Turn right, down the road, towards North Waltham church.

Just past the church, turn left and walk down to the village green and pond, attractively surrounded by half-timbered, thatched cottages. Follow the lane as it curves right for about half a mile to a footpath sign on the left set back a few yards from the turning. Take this beautiful wide way which runs through the fringe of tall trees over the downs. You are now walking along one of those special 'hedgerows' described by Edward in his *Memoir* as 'the chief beauty of Steventon' ... 'an irregular border of copse-wood and timber, often wide enough to contain within it a winding footpath or cart track'. Jane sets a memorable scene in *Persuasion* in a hedgerow like this. The heroine Anne, sitting in a field beyond, overhears a conversation between her former lover, Captain Wentworth, and her rival, Louisa, who are walking down the central path unaware of her presence. Our path leads down to a small pine wood. Bear right, with the wood on

'The chief beauty of Steventon' — a double hedgerow

your right and walk down the field ahead to emerge on the main A30 road by a footpath sign.

Turn right and walk the short distance to the Sun Inn. Opposite the inn, turn left and follow the road (which soon becomes a pleasant lane) to Dummer. Pass a road junction and keep straight on past the pond and the village well until you see the entrance to Dummer church on the right. This twelfth-century church is one of the highlights of the walk. It is full of what John Betjeman called 'rustic cottagey interest' with its seventeenth-century gallery supported by massive oak beams, and rare medieval rood canopy. To the right of the entrance a narrow stair leads to the bellringer's loft and the gallery. The timbers are so thick that it is thought they may have been salvaged from a ship or even be part of what was once a Saxon wooden church.

The white manor house, almost behind the church, was well known to Jane Austen as the home of the Terry family. Although, in one of her letters, she describes them as 'noisy' she also records dancing five times with Stephen Terry at a county ball. Stephen, just a year older than Jane, tells many stories of country life in his fascinating *Diaries of Dummer*. One foggy day, he and a friend lost themselves while shooting woodcock in the New Forest. They were rescued by their resourceful wives who caused the bells of Brockenhurst church to be rung! Stephen's son, Seymour, married Jane's cousin, Georgie Lefroy.

From the church, turn left and walk back through the village to the junction with the road to the Candovers. Turn left and follow this road through attractive rolling country-

The Wheatsheaf Inn on the corner of Popham Lane

side, to a T junction. Turn right for North Waltham. Walk under the motorway and cross the A30 to the Wheatsheaf Inn. This hotel was an important posting-house during the days of the stage coach. Jane walked here to collect the family mail, from North Waltham, down the road to the left of the Wheatsheaf called Popham Lane. As the recipient, she would pay for their letters which, on 11 February 1801, contained one from Charles 'written last Saturday from off the *Start*, and conveyed to Popham Lane by Captain Boyle in his way to Midgham'.

Walk up Popham Lane to North Waltham. Pass the pond on your right, then retrace our route to the church. Turn right by the church along the way we came, left at the footpath sign over the fields, then through the wood to Steventon church.

Map 1

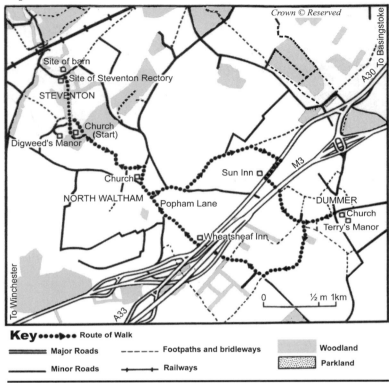

Key ••••▶•• Route of Walk

══════ Major Roads   – – – – – Footpaths and bridleways   ▓▓ Woodland

─────── Minor Roads   +––––+ Railways   ░░ Parkland

From Steventon church walk down lane to see site of rectory. Return and follow footpath sign on left just before the church, making for corner of churchyard rails. Bear half right towards a pine wood. Cross stile on right and keep ahead. Cross stile, bear left and walk down field (fence on left), bear right, then cross stile on left. Walk down field (hedge on right), over stile, up field ahead to stile leading to minor road. Turn right to North Waltham church. Here, turn left to walk down village, then left following lane to Dummer. After about a quarter of a mile follow footpath sign on left. At a small pine wood, bear right (wood on right) to footpath sign by A30. Turn right along main road to Sun Inn. Take road opposite to Dummer. Walk as far as church and manor, then retrace steps to junction with the road to the Candovers. Turn left down this road to T junction. Turn right for North Waltham, go under motorway, over A30 to Wheatsheaf Inn. Follow lane to left of inn to North Waltham. Retrace route to church, turning right before the church, and left at footpath sign along original route back to Steventon church. Distance: about seven miles, very easy walking.

2

Steventon — Visiting Friends and Seeing 'The Neighbourhood'

'The prettiest, silliest, most affected, husband-hunting butterfly' that ever she remembered. That was how Mary Mitford's mother described Jane Austen, from her home at Alresford, not far away. Jane would probably have laughed heartily at this character sketch, more like her own Isabella Thorpe in *Northanger Abbey* than the creator of such a person! She did not take herself, or her friends, too seriously. As she writes to Cassandra: 'Whenever I fall into misfortune, how many jokes it ought to furnish to my acquaintance in general, or I shall die dreadfully in their debt for entertainment.' And she would possibly admit there could be some grounds for such an opinion. The Austens had a wide circle of friends and acquaintances. Jane, attractive and lively, was very fond of dancing and seldom short of partners. On one occasion, even Cassandra, half-joking one suspects, scolds her for flirting. But Jane would regret that she had been misjudged by even one neighbour. The collective voice of local public opinion — what she terms 'the neighbourhood' — is strongly heard in her novels. Her characters, for reasons that vary with their approach to society, are always aware that 'every man is surrounded by a neighbourhood of voluntary spies' as Henry Tilney informs Catherine in *Northanger Abbey*.

Jane portrays the fickle nature of public opinion through the changing attitudes of the society of Meryton in *Pride and Prejudice*. After Jane Bennet's engagement to the highly eligible Mr Bingley 'the Bennets were speedily pronounced to be the luckiest family in the world, though only a few weeks before, when Lydia had first run away, they had been generally proved to be marked out for misfortune'. Jane is so clever at suggesting this background of gossip that she does not need to tell us what Meryton thought of Elizabeth Bennet's engagement; we can easily guess! Jane's letters reveal how her own 'acquaintances' sharpened her taste for irony. 'Mrs Portman is not much admired in Dorsetshire; the good-natured world, as usual, extolled her beauty so highly, that all the neighbourhood have had the pleasure of being disappointed.'

But Jane knew how important it was in their close-knit society to preserve a good name. Lydia Bennet must marry Wickham and become 'respectable' or her whole family, even their 'connections', would suffer. The difficulties and dangers of life — the misery that could be caused by making the wrong choice either wilfully or by mistake — were keenly apparent to someone as clear-eyed as Jane Austen. At times her family commented on her gravity. After the death of a local shopkeeper she wrote to Cassandra that at first the neighbourhood had been deeply affected. But now everyone remarks 'her things were so very dear'. Jane comments: 'Not even death itself can fix the friendship of the world.'

But Jane, like her Elizabeth Bennet who expresses the same feelings, was formed for happiness. She is content to let 'other pens dwell on the guilt and misery'. Through the externals of human behaviour — the anxieties of common life and everyday small concerns — she reveals her characters' inner world, their emotions, desires, strengths and weaknesses. Where these worlds conflict, duty demands one sort of behaviour, inclination another, Jane reveals the situation with delightful irony. Catherine Morland, innocent and loyal to her friend, is sure Henry Tilney is describing Isabella Thorpe as he says to his sister, Eleanor: 'Prepare for your sister-in-law . . . open, candid, artless, guileless, with affections strong but simple, forming no pretensions, and knowing no disguise.'

Unlike Eleanor, who smiles, she does not realise this could never describe the shallow Isabella, even less that Henry could be painting a picture of her own character!

Jane had several good friends near Steventon whom she visited frequently and whose dinners, parties and dances she attended. Even 'acquaintances' could claim their share of her time as the paying and receiving of calls was a social obligation; a quarter-of-an-hour was the minimum politeness demanded. With friends she attended the balls held in the Angel Inn at Basingstoke, the yearly great ball given by the Portsmouths at Hurstbourne Park, and other balls given by the Boltons at Hackwood and the Dorchesters at Greywell and Kempshott. All this society provided her with chances to observe human nature. She was careful never to copy individuals, for her that would be what she termed 'an invasion of social proprieties'. She adds: 'Besides I am too proud of my gentlemen to admit that they are only Mr A or Colonel B.'

This walk follows the paths and lanes Jane Austen took to visit some of her closest friends at Ashe and Deane. We start from Steventon church, as for our first walk, and the distance round is about five miles. From the church, walk a few yards down the lane towards the village. Pass the drive to Steventon manor on your left and immediately after, turn left down the track marked with a footpath sign. Follow the track past the north side of the manor. Just past the manor, over the field on your right, you see the rounded outline of a small copse. Our path runs to the right of these trees. Leave the track to cross a stile over the fence on your right and walk over the field towards the copse, keeping a fence on your left. Walk straight ahead down the side of the field to a minor road by a footpath sign. Turn right and walk down the road towards Steventon. You pass the lane to the site of the rectory (Walk 1) and, on your left, some charming old cottages which Jane knew, Elmtree cottages. Just past these cottages turn left and follow the footpath sign along the edge of the field ahead, keeping the hedge on your right. Climb a flight of wooden steps to cross the railway. Go down the embankment and keep straight on along the edge of the field ahead. Another of these typical Steventon 'hedgerows', a colourful ribbon of oak trees, hawthorns, wild roses and honeysuckle, runs beside our path on the right. Beyond the hedge, the fields roll down to a large plantation of pines. A cart track joins our way on the right. Keep straight on, with a wood fringed with oaks and coppiced hazels on the right and a nursery of young trees on the left.

Our path now bears left to follow the rails of Ashe Park which at first lie behind a belt of pines. Keep the pines close on your right at first then keep ahead over the grass with the drive to Ashe Park about 100 yards away through the trees on your right. Continue to a small wooden gate marked with a footpath sign on your right. Go through the gate and keep straight ahead with a fence close on your left. The drive to Ashe Park runs parallel with our path on the right. Jane would have followed the drive to Ashe Park to visit her friends, the Holders. You can seen the large, red brick mansion, dating back to the days of James I beyond the drive. She tells of several quiet evenings spent here like the one she describes in a letter to Cassandra written in November 1800: 'We had a very pleasant day on Monday at Ashe; we sat down fourteen to dinner in the study, the dining room being not habitable from the storm's having blown down its chimney . . . there was whist and a casino table . . . Rice and Lucy made love, Mat Robinson fell asleep, James and Mrs Augusta alternately read Dr Jenner's pamphlet on the cow pox, and I bestowed my company by turns on all.' The Holders passed their newspaper on to the Austens. Earlier in November, James tells Cassandra: 'Mr Holder's paper tells us that some time in last August Captain Austen (Frank) and the *Peterel* were very active in securing a Turkish ship . . . from the French.' Receiving news of their brothers, almost by chance, must have caused Jane and Cassandra many a sleepless night.

Continue beside the fence. After about a quarter of a mile you will see a small wooden gate on the left marked by a yellow arrow footpath sign. Turn left, through the gate and cross the field ahead bearing half right as the footpath sign indicates to a footpath sign and stile on the other side. Cross the stile to a minor road. Turn right, cross the B3400, and walk up the lane ahead to Ashe. Close to the road on the left you see a beautifully proportioned Georgian house with a delicate fanlight over the door surmounted by a classical pediment. This is Ashe House where one of Jane's closest friends, Mrs Lefroy, lived. Mrs Lefroy, attractive and warm-hearted, was the rector's wife and some years older than Jane. How much Jane loved and admired her can be seen from the poem she wrote, four years after her friend's death in a riding accident. Jane praises her

> genuine warmth of heart without pretence,
> And purity of mind that crowns the whole.

Mrs Lefroy was an excellent hostess and very fond of giving dances. The dividing doors between the morning and dining rooms at Ashe House could be thrown back to allow plenty of room. It was here that Jane met an Irish nephew of Mrs

Ashe House

Lefroy, Tom. She wrote to Cassandra: 'He is a very gentle-manlike, good-looking, pleasant young man, I assure you.' News of Jane's flirting with him at a ball at Manydown drew reproof from Cassandra. Jane writes back teasingly to tell her what happened at the next ball: 'I am almost afraid to tell you how my Irish friend and I behaved. Imagine to yourself everything most profligate and shocking in the way of dancing and sitting down together . . . he is so excessively laughed at about me at Ashe, that he is ashamed of coming to Steventon, and ran away when we called on Mrs Lefroy a few days ago.' Jane writes she is expecting Tom to propose any time and she might accept him if he gives away his light-coloured coat! But her approach seems so light-hearted, it is difficult to believe this affair was very serious. Tom went back to make his fortune in Ireland, eventually becoming Lord Chief Justice, and, after a few inquiries, Jane found other dancing partners. But many years later, Tom Lefroy commented on Jane's charm and added he did love her, but with 'a boy's love'. The present owner of the house pointed out the yew hedge which you can see bordering the garden on the right and told me that one evening Tom Lefroy and Jane left the house to walk in its shelter. When they came back it seemed to everyone that the relationship that had been developing between them was over.

Just beyond Ashe House — it ceased to be a rectory in 1905 — you come to Ashe church which was rebuilt in 1877. As you approach the building, the Lefroy graves are on the right. At the eastern corner a cross marks the grave of Lieu-tenant Robert Portal, of Her Majesty's 5th Royal Irish Lancers, one of the survivors of the charge of the Light Brigade at Balaclava, 1854. The chancel screen inside the church is a careful reproduction of a fifteenth-century original. While the workmen were restoring the church, a robin built its nest on top of the screen out of wood shavings left by the carpenters. In the south wall, west of the screen, is a small square hole closed with a little iron door in which you will see a carving of a robin sitting on its nest. In the

View of Deane

valley south of the church is the source of the river Test.

Opposite the church take the signed footpath. Keep straight on with a fence on the right through a thin belt of woodlands to cross a stile. Walk ahead over a large field aiming for the left-hand corner of a strip of woodland. As you near the woods, look for a gap leading to a path through the trees, about a hundred yards from the left-hand corner. You leave the wood over a stile by a footpath sign shaded by an enormous craggy elm. Ahead of you, across a lovely green, you will see Deane Church. Make your way over the green heading for the right-hand side of the church to cross a stile into a lane by the church gate. Turn right and walked down the lane past a magnificent eighteenth-century mansion with a formal garden approached by a flight of scalloped steps. This is Deane House where Jane visited the Harwood family and attended their dances. Henry Fielding, a novelist she admired although she could not quite forgive him for what she called his low standard of morals, is said to have depicted a member of the Harwood family as the blustering Squire Weston in his *Tom Jones*. The Austen family shared the Harwoods' concern over their rather wild son, Earle. Jane writes that a recent wound he had received was caused by a gun going off accidentally and was not the result of a duel, but the incident was 'again giving uneasiness to his family and talk to the neighbourhood'.

Deane House

Turn right from the entrance to Deane House and walk to the B3400 at Deane Gate. On the right is the site of the rectory. Jane's father was presented with the living of Deane as well as Steventon but from 1790–2 the house was the home of more of her closest friends, Martha and Mary Lloyd, who lived there with their widowed mother. When James' first wife, Anne Mathew, died in 1795, he married Mary Lloyd and came to live at Deane rectory. Martha and her mother were now living at Ibthorpe. In November 1798 Mary was expecting her first child. Jane writes to tell Cassandra (often away staying with Edward in Kent) of the baby's safe arrival. She has been over to see Mary who is making a good recovery but of the child who was asleep she 'had only a glimpse . . . but Miss Debary (the nurse) told me his eyes were large dark and handsome'. So Jane announces the birth of James Edward, always a favourite nephew, and the author of her *Memoir.* Jane shows her mischief in a brief sketch of Miss Debary. (We must remember these were private letters intended only for Cassandra.) '*She* looks much as she used to do, is netting herself a gown in worsteds, and wears what Mrs Birch would call a *pot hat.*'

For the christening of James Edward, Jane decides she must have a new dress. The buying of materials and the making of clothes on a limited income is a frequent topic in her letters. In her novels, Jane loves to show how people reveal their character by the way they shop. No one could fail to recognise Mrs Palmer in *Sense and Sensibility* 'whose eye was caught by everything pretty, expensive, or new; who was wild to buy all, could determine on none, and dawdled away her time in rapture and indecision.'

Cross the road to Deane Gate, past the old posting inn where Charles was once unlucky enough to find the coach full and had to return to Steventon. (If you would like to see a picture of the Deane Gate posting inn as it was in Jane's time the landlord will show you a hundred-year-old photograph on the wall of the bar.) Walk down the lane ahead. Opposite Cheesedown Farm turn left following the byway sign. Jane's father once sent her brother Edward a pig from Cheesedown. Follow the byway uphill until you pass a small wood. Turn right here. (The signpost on the left indicates our direction on the reverse of the post.) Continue beside a field with the wood on your right. Over on the left, you will see the park surrounding Hilsea College, Oakley Hall in Jane's time and the home of her friends, the Bramstons. Jane tells Cassandra about a walk to Oakley Hall in October, 1800: 'At Oakley Hall we did a great deal – eat some sandwiches all over mustard, admired Mr Bramston's porter and Mrs Bramston's transparencies, and gained a promise from the latter of two roots of heartsease, one all yellow and the other all purple, for you.'

Two miles north of Oakley was Manydown Hall, the home of Jane's friends, Alethea, Elizabeth and Catherine Bigg. Their brother, Harris (who took the name Bigg-Wither), the heir to Manydown, proposed to Jane in 1802. She accepted in the evening, but then, realising perhaps that she did not really love him, changed her mind in the morning!

The way now goes through a gap in the fence, then through a wood along the top of the railway embankment. Leave the trees to walk downhill to a footpath sign by the minor road to Steventon. Turn left, under the tunnel, to the village. At the junction turn left along the the lane past the site of the old rectory, then right following the sign to Steventon Church.

Key ●●●●▶●● Route of Walk

════════ Major Roads   ─ ─ ─ ─ ─ ─ Footpaths and bridleways   ▓▓▓▓▓ Woodland

──────── Minor Roads   ●━━━━━● Railways   ▒▒▒▒▒ Parkland

From Steventon church walk few yards down lane. Turn left over stile and down lane. Turn right over fence to walk down edge of field to leave small copse on left. Then on to minor road by footpath sign. Turn right for Steventon. Carry straight on past right turn to site of rectory. Just past Elmtree cottages, look for footpath sign and stile on left. Follow it left, up wooden steps, over railway crossing, down the other side and into field ahead. Walk up field ahead, hedge on right, past wood, bear left round rails of Ashe Park. Keep straight ahead over grass parallel with Ashe Park Drive. Go through small gate on right and keep straight ahead close to fence on left. After about a quarter of a mile turn left through gate and bear half-right over field ahead to footpath sign and stile to minor road. Turn right, cross B3400, then up lane to Ashe. Opposite church take signed footpath. Keep straight on, fence on right, through belt of woods. Cross field ahead towards wood, aiming for a gap 100 yards from left-hand corner. Leave wood over stile by footpath sign. Make your way over the green towards Deane Church to cross the stile into a lane. Walk past Deane House to road. Turn right, cross B3400, down Steventon Lane to turn left at bridleway sign by Cheesedown Farm. Follow this uphill and turn right by small wood. Walk along edge of field (wood on right) then along top of railway embankment, and down the hill to footpath sign by Steventon Lane. Turn left, under tunnel, to the village. Turn left down lane past site of rectory, then right to Steventon church.
Distance: about five miles. Easy walking.

3

In the Hampshire Highlands –
Staying with the Lloyds at Ibthorpe

Ibthorpe – Jane Austen always called the village 'Ibthrop' – is a tiny hamlet tucked away in Hampshire's hilly north-west corner, an area often called 'the highlands of Hampshire'. A handful of cottages connect Ibthorpe with Hurstbourne Tarrant, surely one of the south's most beautiful villages. Here, an ancient church is surrounded by clusters of deep-thatched, half-timbered cottages up to their eaves in holly-hocks and roses, and elegant eighteenth-century houses set in smooth green lawns. Through the village runs the little Bourne stream, whose clear waters have cut a valley through the chalk downs above Andover on their way to meet the river Test. Above the gently curving meadows beyond the village, rise steep-wooded hillsides of elm, oak and ash, the famous 'hangers' of Hampshire. Today, this country is still as remote and beautiful as when Jane Austen walked here with her friends Martha and Mary Lloyd. When she once remarked that she thought lovely scenery must be one of the joys of heaven she must have recalled her rambles around Ibthorpe and Hurstbourne Tarrant.

Jane described herself and Martha as being 'desperate walkers'. She had become very friendly with Martha and Mary while they were living with their widowed mother at Deane Rectory. When her brother James was ordained and married Anne, the Lloyds moved to Ibthorpe, early in 1792. As a parting gift, Jane made for Mary a 'housewife', a tiny roll of flowered silk containing needles and thread. This can be seen at Chawton. In the housewife is a tiny pocket containing a slip of paper on which Jane wrote:

> This little bag, I hope, will prove
> To be not vainly made;
> For should you thread and needles want,
> It will afford you aid.

> And, as we are about to part,
> 'Twill serve another end:
> For, when you look upon this bag,
> You'll recollect your friend.

Later in that year, in the September of 1792 when Jane was seventeen, she travelled the sixteen miles from her home at Steventon to visit the Lloyds at Ibthorpe. One of the results of the difficulties and tedium of eighteenth-century travel (seven miles an hour in a stage coach was considered very good going) was that visits to friends some distance away were usually long, sometimes lasting several months. These long visits play an important part in Jane's stories. In *Northanger Abbey* Catherine has been with the Tilneys a month before she feels she should suggest leaving. So Jane, like the characters in her novels, had plenty of time to settle into the ways of the Ibthorpe household and become acquainted with their friends and 'neighbourhood'. She had ample opportunity to extend her knowledge and appreciation of the people around her, a study which, like her own Elizabeth Bennet, she found endlessly fascinating. From Ibthorpe society in particular I believe she observed aspects of the autocratic woman, the bore, and the gossip which were to find expression in her novels. As we walk in her footsteps we shall meet these people too.

Our walk begins from Hurstbourne Tarrant church. Park in front of the church beside the Bourne where the streamside cottages are linked to the road by tiny bridges. The church, apart from its associations with Jane who worshipped here, is full of interest. It dates back to 1180, just when the solid

The Bourne valley from Hurstbourne Hill

Norman style of building with its rounded arch was giving way to the more pointed Early English style. So here there is combination of both. As you enter through the south porch you see the typical zig-zag Norman carving, and each side of the nave, massive Norman pillars support pointed arches.

To the left of the church stands the house which was the parsonage in the eighteenth century. When Jane visited here, the vicar was the Reverend Peter Debary. His daughters, termed by Jane 'the endless Debaries', frequently called on the Lloyds, primed with the latest gossip. In a letter Jane wrote to Cassandra in 1800, she betrays the boredom she sometimes felt during this chatter. 'Three of the Miss Debaries called this morning after my arrival, but I have not yet been able to return their civility; you know it is not an uncommon circumstance in this parish to have the road from Ibthrop to the parsonage much dirtier and more impracticable for walking than the road from the parsonage to Ibthrop.' The humour with which Jane depicts gossips in her novels is revealed by her ironic comment to Cassandra on the news the Debaries are eager to give her. They have all the latest information about Sir Thomas William's bride-to-be, a Miss Wapshire. Jane remarks that the Debaries say Miss Wapshire 'has always been remarkable for the propriety of her behaviour, distinguishing her far above the general class of Town Misses, and rendering her of course very unpopular among them'. (Jane's cousin, Jane Cooper, had been Sir Thomas's first wife.) Far more interesting for Jane must have been a event which occurred in this old church three years previously in 1797, when, Anne having died, James married Mary Lloyd.

We follow Jane's route as she walked back with the Lloyds after Sunday service to Ibthorpe House, about a mile away. She could follow the lane through the village to cross what is now the A343 and continue to Ibthorpe or she may have taken the footpath along the valley which we shall follow.

With the church tower on your right, walk up the path through the graveyard to a gate on your left. Go through to walk beside the Rectory Farm wall. Cross the stile and bearing a little left, walk past a large wooden barn on your left. Follow the footpath you will see leading right for a few yards, then bear left to go through a gate. The path now runs like a narrow green tunnel beside an old tiled wall to lead to the A343. Cross the road and follow the footpath sign immediately ahead. The path comes to an iron gate and now the lovely valley of the Bourne opens before you. Go through the gate and follow the stream ahead through the lush water meadows. In midsummer the cattle browse knee-deep in buttercups beneath enormous elms and the water runs slowly under a floating carpet of white-flowered cress. On the other side of the stream, there are some thatched cottages. A gate leads from the meadows into a lane. Turn left for a few yards then bear right to a minor road. Now turn right to walk round a small horseshoe-shaped cluster of old thatched cottages which is Ibthorpe. The lane bears left to meet the Ibthorpe road and on the corner, on your right, you will see a rose-coloured eighteenth-century house in a beautiful walled garden. This is Ibthorpe House. It is built in the simple, ordered classical style, with near rows of sash windows and a scroll-supported canopy over the front door. The house dates back to Tudor times and the kitchen retains its low-beamed ceiling and diamond-leaded panes. After Mary's marriage, Martha continued to live here with her mother. Before Jane's projected visit in 1800, she suggested to Jane that she should bring some books with her. Jane teases: 'I come to you to be talked to, not to read or hear reading. I can do *that* at home . . .' As ever, Jane shows her delight in people. She promises Martha a potted version of the *History of England* as her share of the conversation. The only other resident at Ibthorpe House was a very dull old lady called Mrs Stent. Jane felt fully the effects of Mrs Stent's company. She continues to Martha: 'With such provision on my part, if you will do yours by repeating the French Grammar and Mrs Stent will now and then ejaculate some wonder about the cocks and hens, what can we want?' She must often have suffered, like Emma who cannot resist the opportunity to be witty at Miss Bates' expense, from the society of this boring old lady. But one of Jane's strongest qualities in her novels is her ability to portray bores as real and interesting people. She felt as great a sympathy with them as she did with her more attractive characters. Two of her most memorable creations are Miss Bates and Mr Woodhouse in *Emma* – and yet both could be almost insufferable bores! Perhaps her knowledge of Mrs Stent inspired her portrait of Mrs Allen in *Northanger Abbey* whose 'vacancy of mind and incapacity for thinking were such, that as she never talked a great deal so she could never be entirely silent; and therefore . . . if she lost her needle or broke her thread, if she heard a carriage in the street, or saw a speck upon her gown, she must observe it aloud . . .'

Turn right in front of Ibthorpe House and follow the lane (passing a turning on the left) until you come to the next track on the left. Take this track as it winds gradually uphill through thickets of hazels and hawthorns, elderberries and wild roses. On your left runs a steep-sided valley and glimpses of wide,

Cottages at Ibthorpe

Ibthorpe House

rolling countryside appear through the trees on your right. Perhaps as Jane walked along these peaceful ways with Martha, her friend told her more about her mother's horrifying upbringing. Jane based the character of Lady Susan, in her novel of that name – possibly her first attempt at a novel and written in letter form about 1793-4 – on Mrs Lloyd's experiences. Her mother, Mrs Craven, was a beauty, and like Lady Susan, shone in society. But she treated her daughters shockingly, locking them up, beating and starving them, until, in desperation, they ran away from home and married. Lady Susan, a self-declared and unashamed adulteress (in a letter Jane remarked: 'I have a good eye for an adulteress'), despises and ill-treats her daughter, neglects her education and tries to force her to marry a rather spineless nobleman. In spite of her cruelty Lady Susan has a certain fascination as she determinedly pursues her own ends, delighting in humbling those who despise her. Although she is to some extent a caricature, her autocratic spirit lives on to appear in various forms in many of Jane's later, more rounded characters. We can hear her voice in that of Lady Catherine in *Pride and Prejudice* as she tries to intimidate Elizabeth: 'I have not been used to submit to any person's whims. I have not been in the habit of brooking disappointment.'

When the path branches to form a Y junction, follow the track as it bears left. At the next Y junction bear right. The way becomes asphalted and drops to a minor road. Turn left along the road to a junction. Now turn left again, following the lane signposted Hurstbourne Tarrant as it runs through open fields over Pill Heath. From this high point you can look over the forest stretching over Windmill Hill down to a patchwork of fields and woods rising and falling to merge into a blue haze on the horizon. Follow this lane for almost two miles as it crosses over the downs with wide views southwards over rolling countryside. In November 1821 William Cobbett, the author of *Rural Rides* and a great campaigner on behalf of the agricultural worker, came over these hills for the sixth time that year to stay at Hurstbourne Tarrant – which he called

'Uphusband' – as the guest of Joseph Blount at Rookery Farm House, near the bridge. (You can still see a brick Cobbett laid in the front wall, incised with his initials.) No doubt he reined in his horse on this road, to meditate upon the prospect before him, judging the lie of the land with his shrewd eye, marking its soils and crops, so later he could harangue the landlords.

When you come to the main road, the A343, go straight across and follow the footpath sign ahead down a narrow path with trees on the right to enter the Forestry Commission's Doles Wood. The path meets a wide green forest track. Bear left and after about fifty yards look for a narrow path on the left marked by a post with three yellow arrow footpath signs. Turn left to follow the central path (at the time of writing the only path visible). The path leads through the trees then drops gently downhill. The great Hampshire naturalist, George Dewar, was born in 1862 at Doles House, close by. He describes this steep wood, dipping down to the Bourne valley as 'the Hanging' and comments on the richness of the wild flowers, particularly the profusion of wild Solomon's Seal. It is still under the trees, its white wax-like flowers hanging like tiny lanterns from its long stems. Keep to the path as it turns left to drop more steeply down the hillside. Ahead, Hurstbourne Tarrant lies beside its meadows, shaded by its rising woodlands.

Keep the woods on your right and walk down the hillside with the church directly ahead. Follow the path as it bears right then left. Cross the school playing fields, go over the Bourne and so back to your car.

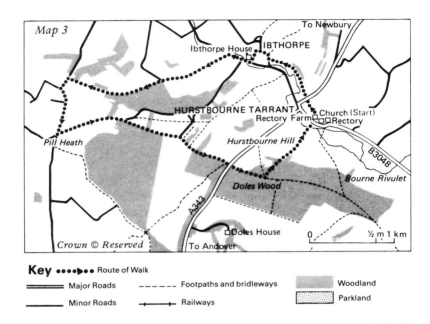

Key •••●>•• Route of Walk

══════ Major Roads   — — — — Footpaths and bridleways   ▨ Woodland

————— Minor Roads   —+—+— Railways   ▨ Parkland

From Hurstbourne Tarrant church, follow footpath to left of tower. Go through gate on left, follow path beside Rectory Farm wall, pass thatched barn, bear right for a few yards, then left through gate. Follow path to A343. Cross road, follow footpath sign ahead to iron gate to meadows beside the Bourne stream. Keep ahead to lane. Turn left for a few yards to minor road. Turn right and walk round horseshoe. When lane meets road turn right in front of Ibthorpe House for about a quarter of a mile, pass track on left, turn left up the next track. At Y junction, bear left and keep ahead following signs. Track now asphalted drops to a minor road. Turn left to a junction, then left again following signpost to Hurstbourne Tarrant. Cross the A343, follow footpath sign immediately ahead beside wood to enter Doles Wood. Meet a wide grassy track. Turn left for about fifty yards. Take narrow footpath on left marked by central yellow arrow footpath sign. Path descends the hill then turns left, hillside on left, trees on right. Hurstbourne Tarrant church is directly ahead. Cross school playing fields, over the Bourne, to church.
Distance: about five miles, Easy walking, hill climbing gradual.

4

With Edward in Kent –
Goodnestone and Rowling

In Jane Austen's novels, no character, however minor, is allowed to float about in an indecisive manner. Although her first concern is always with people and their reactions to one another, her people are always firmly attached to places. If they are inside we know what the room looks like, who else is there, even the view from the windows. If outside, we know the season, the weather, the state of the ground and the appearance of the countryside. Jane conveys this realism without any long descriptions. A precise, exact touch of colour at just the right place in her story is all she needs. When, in *Pride and Prejudice*, Elizabeth visits Lady Catherine de Bourgh's home, Rosings, she sees it as 'a handsome modern building, well situated on rising ground'. When she calls she walks 'up the steps to the Hall'. Seeking a quiet retreat, she finds a 'nice sheltered path beside an open grove'. In a delightful way, Jane often makes a character's home illustrate their nature. The appearance of the pompous and unimaginative Mr Collins' parsonage is just what we might expect. Elizabeth, looking eagerly out of the coach windows for her first view of it, sees: 'The garden sloping down to the road, the house standing in it, the green pales and the laurel hedge'.

Jane places Rosings and Mr Collins' parsonage in Kent. Early in the story, a letter from Mr Collins is dated from 'Hunsford, near Westerham, Kent'. Jane began writing *Pride and Prejudice* about October 1796 when she was twenty, and only a few weeks before she had made a similar journey to that of her heroine Elizabeth to visit her brother, Edward, who lived at Rowling, near Goodnestone, a few miles southeast of Canterbury. As her coach rattled along the road on its three-day journey from Steventon, her mind must have been busy devising the people and places she was to portray in the story. Many of her realistic touches I am sure were inspired by Rowling, and nearby Goodnestone House, the elegant home of Sir Brook and Lady Bridges, the parents of Elizabeth, Edward's wife. Certainly we can recognise traits from the characters of some of the people Jane met on this visit in several of the lively folk who emerge from the pages of *Pride and Prejudice*.

The story of Jane's third brother, Edward, is more like a tale from one of the romantic novels all the Austens enjoyed reading than real life. Adopted as a child by wealthy relatives, the Knights, he was brought up in Kent as the heir to Godmersham and other large estates. After making his Grand Tour abroad, he met and fell in love with the beautiful and sweet-natured daughter of a baronet. Elizabeth's parents offered the young couple a small house at Rowling, about a mile from Goodnestone. When Jane visited them in 1796, Edward and Elizabeth already had three small children. The eldest, Fanny, was to become specially dear to her Aunt Jane, 'almost another sister' Jane called her, the highest compliment she could pay. In her lively letters to Cassandra, Jane reveals a great deal of her reactions to Kent and the people she met. Jane travelled with her brothers, Edward and Frank, and like her heroine Elizabeth Bennet, broke her journey in London. From a hotel in Cork Street, she writes merrily: 'Here I am once more in this scene of dissipation and vice, and I begin already to find my morals corrupted!' Driving across Kent, they would go by way of Sevenoaks, Maidstone and Canterbury and pass through a village called 'Westerham'. Pembury and Lamberhurst remind us of more place-names in *Pride and Prejudice*, Darcy's home, 'Pemberley' close to the village of 'Lambton'. (It is unlikely Jane had a Derbyshire house in mind.)

This walk in the lanes around Goodnestone House and village to Rowling, follows Jane's footsteps as she frequently walked between the two households. The distance round is about three miles. (Footpaths in this part of Kent are not well marked, but the lanes in this lovely and remote country-side are very pleasant walking.) For this walk, and the next around Godmersham, Canterbury makes the ideal centre.

The Christchurch Gate, Canterbury

Jane knew this ancient town well. When Mrs Knight left Godmersham to Edward, she retired to 'White Friars', her house in the Close in Canterbury. Jane called on her there, and sometimes stayed overnight. Edward, as a visiting magistrate, attended the Canterbury courts and in November, 1813, she toured the town jail with him. She wrote to Cassandra sadly: 'I went through all the feelings which people must go through I think in visiting such a building'.

Our starting place is the church in Goodnestone village. From Canterbury, follow the A257 east, in the direction of Wingham. Just past the church in Wingham, turn south along the B2046 for about a mile and a half, before taking the left turn for Goodnestone. Drive through the village and the church is on your right, past the Fitzwalter Arms. Park under the shade of tall elms and chestnuts. Goodnestone village is a tiny cluster of latticed and gabled cottages built in similar style of soft red brick, sheltered in a wooded fold of the downs. Ancient records call the village 'Godwineston' from Earl Godwin who owned the land before the Norman Conquest. During the reign of Queen Anne the estate passed to the Bridges family who rebuilt the great house, and later, parts of the village. The delightful village shop and post office dates from 1757. Today, there are few changes, and we see Goodnestone very much as Jane saw it. Cross the road to the Church of the Holy Cross. Jane would recognise the tower, part of its lower stages dates from the twelfth century, but not the present nave and chancel as these were rebuilt in 1839–41. However, she would have known the beautiful late medieval north aisle with its large black and white memorial to the first Brook Bridges, the ancestor of her sister-in-law. With her eye for perfection in detail – 'an artist can do nothing slovenly' she once wrote – she must have loved the exquisite outlines and jewel colourings of the medieval glass in some of the windows. We felt too she would have enjoyed the delicacy of the sixteenth- and seventeenth-century brasses below the east window.

Turn right at the church gate and follow the lane ahead.

Goodnestone village

At first you walk between banks of hazels and elderberries, twined with wild clematis, but then the hedge to the left gives way to wide views over rolling parkland dotted with fine elms. Go through a white gate into Goodnestone Park. The path crosses the park with a high garden wall on the right which masks your view of the house at this point. But even from this path you will be able to glimpse a little of its classical elegance, its ordered rows of sash windows above a pillared porch surmounted by a triangular pediment. (Later we have a better view.) Jane often called at Goodnestone House to exchange news, dine, and meet friends. In a letter she records a particularly happy evening when it was her privilege to open a ball with Edward Bridges. 'We dined at Goodnestone and in the evening danced two country dances and the boulangeries,' she writes. 'Elizabeth played one country dance, Lady Bridges the other.' We can imagine the brightly-lit rooms full of laughter and music and Jane,

A group of waltzers, 1817, engraved for La Belle Assemblée. *The Victoria and Albert Museum, London*

elegant in her high-waisted gown and satin slippers, feeling, like Catherine Morland in *Northanger Abbey*, 'her spirits dance within her'. Jane reflects her own love of dancing in the many ballroom scenes in her novels. Of course, they gave her splendid opportunities for presenting her characters and revealing differing aspects of them but the genuine delight that her heroines experience in a ball, in contemplating the event beforehand and in reliving it afterwards, must surely be Jane's own. When, after a ball, Emma Watson remarks sorrowfully 'how soon it is at an end! I wish it could come all over again!' she is echoing her creator. After the dancing at Goodnestone, there was supper and then Jane tells Cassandra 'we walked home at night under the shade of two umbrellas'.

Jane met much varied company at Goodnestone and the future novelist allowed her imagination full play. 'We dine today at Goodnestone,' she writes, 'to meet my Aunt Fielding from Margate, and a Mr Clayton, her professed admirer; at least so I imagine.' Most interesting of all was a visit she paid with her relatives to Nackington, a large house, two miles south of Canterbury. Here she met a Miss Fletcher who, in spite of the fact that she was wearing purple muslin 'which did not become her complexion' had two pleasing traits: 'she admires *Camilla* and drinks no cream in her tea'. Evidently, a Steventon friend, Lucy Lefroy, had been friendly with Miss Fletcher while on a visit to Canterbury and been expecting a letter from her. Jane writes that she mentions this but 'Miss Fletcher says in her defence that as everybody Lucy knew when she was in Canterbury, has now left it, she has nothing at all to write to her about. By *Everybody*, I suppose that a new set of officers have arrived there. But this is a note of my own.' A note we recognise in the foolish, weak-minded Lydia Bennet in *Pride and Prejudice* flirting with the militia officers billeted in Meryton and unable to take pleasure in the company of any man who did not wear a scarlet coat. Like Miss Lefroy, Jane is expecting a letter. James had promised to write with news of a ball. 'After this

Goodnestone House

time he must have collected his ideas enough,' she writes. We recall Mr Bennet asking his dull and bookish daughter Mary for her opinions on social etiquette. When Mary is slow to answer, Mr Bennet remarks, 'While Mary is adjusting her ideas ... let us return to Mr Bingley...'

Jane enjoyed walking through Goodnestone Park. One day she took Frank to Crixhall Ruff, a wood to the north of the park. During a later visit to Goodnestone, in August, 1805, she writes to Cassandra: 'Walked to Rowling ... and very great was my pleasure in going over the house and grounds. We have also found time to visit all the principal walks of this place, except the walk round the top of the park, which we shall accomplish probably today.' We plan to follow her footsteps to Rowling. Go past the lodge at the park gates and turn left down the lane. You pass a very beautiful half-timbered farmhouse, Bonnington Farm, on your right. Our lane bears left past a turning to Aylesham to a lane on the right leading to Chillenden. We turn right here, along this lane, but before doing so, look left through a gap in the trees for a splendid view of Goodnestone House on the slope of the opposite hillside. Like Rosings, Jane could well describe it as 'a fine modern house', with all its dignity well able to inspire Mr Collins with feelings of humble and respectful alarm!

Turn right and follow the quiet lane to Chillenden. You walk past woods of slim-leaved Spanish chestnuts and between open wheatfields. As the lane dips between high, bramble-covered banks, you will see the roofs of the village ahead and the angled cones of oast houses surrounded by their hop fields. Beyond the fields rise wooded slopes. Just before you reach the village you come to a crossroads. Turn left here and follow the lane which now crosses flatter countryside. To the right you pass a conspicuous wooden postmill with white sails. This mill for grinding corn is connected to a wheel so that the whole device can be turned round to make the most favourable use of the wind. Behind the postmill, over the fields, you will see a wooded copse which conceals all but a glimpse of Rowling House. When you reach the next crossroads, turn right to walk over the flat countryside towards Rowling. Large, open fields stretch away to the horizon giving wide views almost to the sea. And seagulls perched among the stubble of the newly-harvested corn reminded us of the sea's closeness. The scene cannot have changed very much since Jane walked this way over a hundred and eighty years ago. Bear left at the fork and follow it to the wood surrounding Rowling. The drive, the popular curved 'sweep' of Jane's day, leads from the lane, on the left, and through the trees you can glimpse the house. It is easy to picture from her letters, how Jane spent her time here. 'I am very happy here,' she writes. She enjoyed playing with the children and little George seems a special favourite. 'I have taken little George once in my arms since I have been here, which I thought very kind,' she jokes to Cassandra. She seems to have been seldom idle. When not engaged with company, the ladies sewed. 'We are very busy making Edward's shirts,' she comments. She kept up her daily practice at the piano and she read. She took a keen interest in all the family's activities, noting how much Frank was enjoying his visit. As became a sailor, Frank was clever with his fingers and makes a toy wooden butter churn for Fanny. For the gentlemen of course, a great deal of the time was taken up in shooting, the season having just begun. Henry joins the Goodnestone party to enjoy the sport. Jane reports: 'They say there are a prodigious number of birds hereabouts this year, so that perhaps *I* may kill a few.' Evidently the chance or even the possibility of Jane managing to hit a bird was extremely remote. Killing, of any kind, seems quite foreign to her nature. Death is almost absent from her novels. She comments rather witheringly on her brother's sport. 'Edward and Fly (Frank) went out yesterday very early in a couple of shooting jackets, and came home like a couple of bad shots for they killed nothing at all. They are out again today, and are not yet returned. Delightful sport! They are just come home; Edward with his two brace, Frank with his two and a half. What amiable young men!' But Jane recognised the importance of shooting in the life of a country gentleman. The most admirable of the gentlemen in her novels shoot. We recall Mrs Bennet, anxious to win a suitor for her daughter Jane, telling the new young owner of Netherfield, 'When you have killed all your own birds, Mr Bingley . . . I beg you will come here, and shoot as many as you please on Mr Bennet's manor.'

Retrace your steps to the crossroads. Cross straight over and follow the lane towards Goodnestone. Go straight over the next crossroads and walk down the hill with the park on your left. Ahead, there is a lovely view of the village in its wooded valley and the church a little higher up the hillside. When you reach the village, turn left to walk the short distance back to the church. Today, Goodnestone is still a peaceful and remote place, retaining its eighteenth-century atmosphere. Life in so retired a spot as Goodnestone was soon to cease for Edward and Elizabeth and their young family. Shortly after Jane returned to Steventon to write *Pride and Prejudice* (or *First Impressions* as she called the novel at first) Edward moved with his family to the house where he had been brought up, the great house at Godmersham. When she visited there, Jane enjoyed a new kind of life as sister of a wealthy country gentleman, now master of great estates with a wide social and political influence. In our next walk we follow Jane to Godmersham.

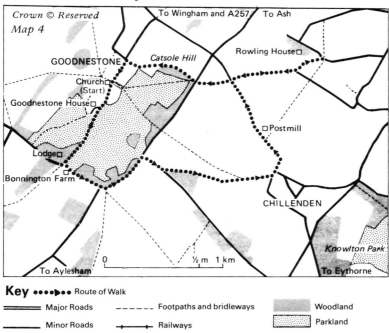

Crown © Reserved
Map 4

Key ●●●▶●● Route of Walk

═══════ Major Roads   _____ Footpaths and bridleways   ▓▓▓ Woodland

─────── Minor Roads   ┼───┼ Railways   ░░░ Parkland

From Canterbury follow A257 to Wingham. Past church, turn south along B2046 for about a mile and a half, take left turn for Goodnestone. Park opposite church. With back to church, turn right and follow lane, through a white gate, across Goodnestone Park. At lodge gates turn left, then right in the direction of Chillenden. Pass post mill. At crossroads turn right for Rowling. Retrace steps to crossroads. Go straight over, then over next crossroads towards Goodnestone village, with park on left. Then turn left to walk through Goodnestone village back to the church.
Distance: about three miles, very easy walking.

5

Godmersham

When the wealthy but childless Knights of Godmersham Park decided to adopt an heir for their estates they could not have made a better choice than Edward Austen. He proved sensible, practical, a good landlord and caring father. Mrs Knight, after the death of her husband, could feel justified in retiring to Canterbury and leaving the administration of the great house to Edward and his lovely Elizabeth. For Cassandra, devoted to Edward, Godmersham became almost a second home and Jane was a frequent visitor. But although Jane revelled in the luxury of Godmersham: 'Kent is the only place for happiness!' she wrote, 'everyone is rich there!' she was never happy for long away from her own Hampshire home. Writing from Godmersham she retails all the family news to Cassandra, she describes dinners, dances and visits, and as always, her sharp eyes observe telling details of the folk she met. Among these we can find hints for the character of Darcy in *Pride and Prejudice*, for Miss Bates and Mrs Elton in *Emma*. The setting of Godmersham, within a curve of the Stour and framed by the wooded hillsides, possibly suggested Darcy's home, Pemberley, to Jane. More important, her knowledge of life in a great house, and the social impact of Godmersham found expression in her profound novel *Mansfield Park*. Jane is sometimes accused of avoiding the deeper social and moral issues of her time, but in this novel, beneath the tender love story, lies a bitter conflict between the old ways, of which

Mansfield Park is a symbol, and the new, personified by the London-bred Mary and Henry Crawford.

This short walk, about three miles in length, takes us to Godmersham and over the Park to climb to the North Downs Way. From Canterbury follow the A28 down the pleasant valley of the Stour. The river runs between rounded hillsides rising above orchards and hop fields. After about eight miles, the road takes you through Godmersham village. Look for the church on a green slope beyond the river on the right. Turn right down the lane just past the church and you will find room to park by the church gates. You can arrive by bus from Canterbury which stops in the village. Walk down the main road to the turning on the right for the church. When she stayed at Godmersham, Jane worshipped here in this little church dedicated to St Lawrence beside the Stour. Recorded history, dating back to AD 824, proves that this settlement by the river has been a popular site from earliest times. This feeling of antiquity is confirmed by the church with its semicircular apse lit by Norman windows. On the right of the nave is a memorial to Thomas and Catherine Knight who adopted Edward. Edward later took the name of Knight which seems to have been quite a usual practice. In *Emma*, Mr Weston's son Frank is adopted by the wealthy Churchill family as their heir and arrives in Highbury as 'Frank Churchill'. On the opposite side of the nave, Edward and Elizabeth have their memorial. In the graveyard, on the banks of the Stour, you will find the grave of Sackree, their children's nurse. She lived to the age of ninety and was loved by all. Jane mentions her several times with affection in her letters.

From the church, turn right and walk along the lane. The wall of Godmersham Park runs beside you on your left. On the right, through a screen of sycamores and elderberries you overlook the wide valley of the Stour. Opposite the point where the land bends right to a bridge over the river, you will see two sets of park gates either side of a lodge on your left. This is the entrance to Godmersham Park. The grounds are

private, but a beautiful and well-marked footpath runs from just inside the second set of gates, right, over the grass, then up the hillside ahead. Go through the impressive gates and look immediately right and you will see a footpath sign by a small wooden gate. Go through the gate and keep straight ahead over the park through a beautiful circle of trees to another gate on your left. Turn left to go through the gate and follow the wide grassy path between fences all the way uphill. Now, as you climb, you have a wonderful view of Gomersham House on the left, beside the Stour, looking down the valley and framed by its sloping meadows, woods and copses. Built early in the eighteenth century, it is a long low building on the plan of a Roman villa with a central hall and two wings. The north front, which we can see, has typical, classical-inspired triangular pediments over the door and neat rows of windows. In *Pride and Prejudice*, Elizabeth Bennet sees Pemberley for the first time as we see Godmersham, from the hillside. 'Situated on the opposite side of a valley – it was a large, handsome stone building, standing well on rising ground, and backed by a range of woody hills.' And, like Godmersham, Pemberley has a stream winding through its grounds. As we look down the valley we can share Elizabeth's delight in the view from its windows: 'Every disposition of the ground was good; and she looked on the whole scene, the river, the trees scattered on its banks, and the winding of the valley ... with delight.'

Jane had visited Godmersham as early as 1798 with her parents and sister. Cassandra was left behind when they returned at the end of October and when they broke their return journey at Dartford Jane wrote with news of the travellers. Beneath the heading 'The Bull and George Inn' she comments that her father is reading a novel from the library and her mother resting by the fire. The weather had been good. A shower upon leaving Sittingbourne had been followed by 'a very bright *chrystal* afternoon'. Cassandra was still at

Left: Godmersham church reflected in the placid waters of the Stour

Godmersham in December, and Jane writes teasingly from Steventon, contrasting their simple life at the rectory with that at Godmersham: 'We dine now at half after three, and have done dinner I suppose before you begin — We drink tea at half after six. I am afraid you will despise us.' In Jane's novels, mealtimes reveal the social standing of her characters. The later you ate your dinner, the more aristocratic you considered yourself. In the country, gentry like old-fashioned Mr Woodhouse in *Emma*, still enjoyed their dinner soon after three. The village ladies who spent the evenings with him and kept similar hours, were ready, if he was not, for a substantial supper later. But, possibly owing to the late hours of Parliament, the fashionable would dine as late as six or seven, as did the Netherfield ladies in *Pride and Prejudice* and the Godmersham family. However, there seems to have been little ostentation at Godmersham. Jane's next comments create a homely picture: 'How do you spend your evenings? — I guess that Elizabeth works (a lady's 'work' was sewing — when Jane refers to her work she does not mean writing!), that you read to her, and that Edward goes to sleep.'

In 1808, it was Jane who was at Godmersham, writing to Cassandra in Southampton. She was met in the Hall by Fanny and her small sister Lizzy, 'with a great deal of pleasant joy' and now she is in her room, the Yellow room. She comments: 'It seems odd to me to have a great place to myself.' Amid the busy social life that Godmersham provided, Jane welcomed the peace and privacy her room afforded, spending two or three hours there after breakfast. She wrote letters; perhaps she made notes for future revisions of her early novels. We find her constantly observing the Godmersham society. 'Nobody ever feels or acts, suffers or enjoys, as one expects,' she tells Cassandra. Like her own Elizabeth Bennet, it was the complicated characters who interested her most. She refers several times, with an insistence that betrays her interest, to Mr Moore, Harriot Bridges' husband, who seems to have much in common with Darcy in *Pride and Prejudice*. We remember Darcy's reserve at the Netherfield

Print: Godmersham House from E. Hasted's Kent, *1799*

Godmersham Park today

Ball and his comment to Elizabeth that 'We neither of us perform to strangers' as Jane tells Cassandra that 'Mr Moore did not talk so much as I expected, and I understand from Fanny, that I did not see him at all as he is in general: — our being strangers made him so much more silent and quiet'. We hear more echoes of Darcy, who so upset the hopeful mothers of the young ladies of Meryton, as Jane comments once more on Mr Moore. He is certainly a gentleman 'but by no means winning — not unagreeable tho' nothing seems to go right with him'. However, she shrewdly observes, 'He is a sensible man and tells a story well.' His awkwardness amused Jane as Darcy amused Elizabeth. A delightful note occurs when Mr Moore has joined Jane and the other ladies for an evening. 'We sat quietly working and talking till 10, when he ordered his wife away, and we adjourned to the dressing room to eat our tart and jelly.' Jane has her doubts about Harriot's happiness and it certainly required a girl of spirit to stand up to Darcy.

Jane, naturally, enjoyed life at Godmersham. 'In another week,' she writes, 'I shall be at home . . . in the meantime for elegance and ease and luxury . . . I shall eat ice and drink French wine, and be above vulgar economy.' But her own home, and the companionship of her beloved sister were of first importance to her. When she returns, household cares await, but 'the pleasures of friendship, of unreserved conversation, of similarity of taste and opinions, will make good amends for orange wine'. These are the standards she stresses in *Mansfield Park*. She completed this novel early in 1813. The importance of Mansfield Park, the great house, is paramount in the story as Jane works out an approach to life in a society she sees to be in a constant state of change and flux. The house represents all that is best in the old order: stability, high moral standards and correctness of behaviour. These were being undermined and challenged by the new ideas of making money at any price and selfish pleasure-seeking. But if some sort of harmony were to be achieved, each side needed the best of the other. Jane saw clearly the weaknesses inherent in the old order; power could lead to corruption or to a mere parade of standards with no real feeling for others or concern for their welfare. We see these faults in the owner of Mansfield Park, Sir Thomas Bertram, his eldest son Tom, and his daughters Julia and Maria. Only his younger son, Edmund, fulfils the old ideals, and he is weak. Fanny joins their family from outside. A poor cousin, she has experienced a different, suffering kind of life which has strengthened her. She is sensitive, imaginative and loving. To survive, against the threat of the new, seductive, but fundamentally corrupt ways of thinking, Mansfield Park needs Fanny who has survived temptation. So Edmund marries Fanny, Mansfield Park has its inheritors; there is hope for the future.

When Jane visited Godmersham for the last time in September, 1813, she was thinking about another story. Less profound perhaps, more amusing but at times, very moving, *Emma*. Her little niece, Marianne, recalls how Aunt Jane 'would sit very quietly at work' beside the library fire, 'then suddenly burst out laughing, jump up, cross the room to a distant table with papers lying on it, write something down, returning presently and sitting down quietly to her work'. Sometimes she would take the older girls and read to them something which produced 'peals of laughter'. How Marianne, on the wrong side of the door, longed to hear these stories! Again, Jane's letters reveal the novelist's approach. She records a certain John Plumtre: 'A handsome young man certainly, with quiet gentlemanlike manners. I set him down as sensible rather than brilliant. There is nobody brilliant nowadays.' Jane endured the usual succession of courtesy calls. 'Lady Eliz. Hatton and Annamaria called here this morning; yes they called, they came and they sat and they went.' But some really interested her, like Miss Milles, a good-hearted chatterer who surely furnished Jane with some hints for that 'great talker upon little matters', Miss Bates in *Emma*. Jane writes: 'Miss Milles was queer as usual . . . she undertook *in three words* to give us the history of Mrs Scudamore's reconciliation, and then talked on about it for half-an-hour, using such odd expressions and so foolishly minute, that I could hardly keep my countenance . . . we may guess how that point will be discussed evening after evening.'

Much less likeable was a Mrs Britton, so similar to Mrs Elton in *Emma*. Mrs Britton, Jane writes, is 'a large, ungenteel woman – with self-satisfied and would-be elegant manners . . . she amuses me very much with her affected elegance and refinement'. We remember Mrs Elton addressing her dear 'Knightley' with her views on strawberry picking and endeavouring to impress the society of Highbury with her sister Selina's magnificent appearance in her barouche-landau.

Jane took great pleasure in exploring the grounds of Godmersham, as her Elizabeth did in those of Pemberley. As we climb, our path reveals more of Godmersham's lovely surroundings. Footpath signs lead us straight on, past the gamekeeper's house on the right. Above the house, go through a gate and take the white chalk path leading uphill a little to your right, past a stand of fine old beech trees towards a line of woodland. From this height you overlook smaller hills crowned with those circular copses planted by eighteenth-century landowners so intent on their 'improvements' and providing shelter for their game. Jane refers to walks she took to look at these. 'Yesterday passed quite a la Godmersham; the gentlemen rode about Edward's farm, and returned in time to saunter along Bentigh (a hill) with us; and after dinner we visited the Temple Plantations. James and Mary are much struck with the beauty of the place ....' On her last visit she comments: 'How Bentigh has grown! – and the Canty Hill Plantation!' It is interesting that all Jane's heroines take pleasure in nature.

The chalk path gives way to grass as you near the top of the hill and becomes indistinct. Bear half right over the grass towards a fence crossed by a stile indicated by a footpath sign. Cross the stile and the field ahead. Follow the narrow path which leads to another stile. Over the stile you come to a wide, green path running through a fringe of woodlands along the hillside. This is a beautiful part of the North Downs Way. If you wish, you could turn right and follow the Way to Chilham, about two miles. This is a charming village with streets of half-timbered houses, a fifteenth-century church and a seventeenth-century castle above the Stour with the keep of a Norman castle in its grounds. Jane visited acquaintances in Chilham and attended balls and concerts at the castle. If you turn right in Chilham and walk the short distance back to the main road you can catch the bus back to Godmersham. Or you can turn left to follow the Way into King's Wood. It is pleasant to think of Jane rambling these paths, thinking perhaps of the characters who were to people her imaginary village of Highbury in *Emma*. The upright Mr Knightley, Jane's ideal of a true gentleman, a wealthy landowner who not only managed his estates well but took a real interest in his tenants and the welfare of his poor, must owe a great deal to her observation of Edward. So Jane's visits to Godmersham helped to shape not only some of the settings and characters in her novels, but the basic philosophy upon which she constructed them.

From King's Wood, retrace your steps from the Way, down the hill and back through the park. After going through the lodge gates turn right to follow the lane back to the church. If you arrived by bus, cross the bridge opposite the lodge gates for a quick way back to the stop in Godmersham village.

The Stour at Godmersham

Map 5

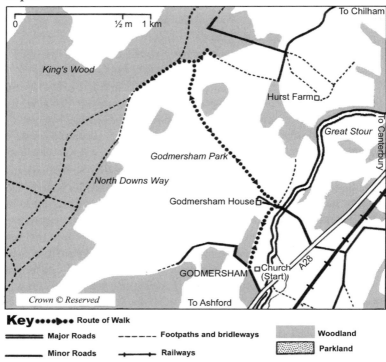

Key •••◗•• **Route of Walk**

═══════ **Major Roads**   — — — — **Footpaths and bridleways**   ░░░░░ **Woodland**

▬▬▬▬▬ **Minor Roads**   ＋—＋—＋ **Railways**   ▒▒▒▒▒ **Parkland**

From Canterbury, follow A28 for about eight miles, through Godmerhsam village. Turn right just past the church and park by church gates. Or catch the bus which stops in Godmersham village. Turn right from church gates and follow lane by wall of Godmersham House to point where the lane bends right to cross the Stour. Go through second set of gates on the left. Turn immediately right to cross the grass to footpath sign by small iron gate. Turn left in direction of sign and walk uphill past the gamekeeper's house. Go through gate, take white chalk path uphill. Near the top path becomes indistinct. Bear half right to fence and cross stile by footpath sign. Cross field and next stile to the North Downs Way running along a fringe of woodland, right to Chilham, left to King's Wood. (It is a lovely walk to Chilham, then would suggest catching the bus back. Turn right in Chilham for the A28.) From the King's Wood retrace your steps from the Way, through the park gates. Turn right for the church. Keep straight on over the bridge for quick way back to Godmersham village.

Distance: about three miles to King's Wood. Five miles to Chilham.

6

Jane visits Bath

As she approaches Bath for the first time the heroine of *Northanger Abbey*, Catherine Morland, is 'all eager delight'. Although happy living in the country, she thoroughly enjoys being caught up in the whirl of fashionable activities that each day in this fascinating city brings her. As she tells Henry Tilney: 'here are a variety of amusements, a variety of things to be seen and done . . . Oh, who can ever be tired of Bath?'

In setting so much of this early novel in Bath, Jane attributes a great many of her own first impressions of the city to its heroine. Like Catherine, Jane came to Bath as a visitor when she was young. She, too, was accustomed to a quiet life in the countryside. A greater contrast with Steventon is hard to imagine. Second only to London, Bath was still the great health and pleasure resort of the wealthy, as famous for its shops, balls, concerts and theatre as it was for its healing springs and medical facilities. To accommodate the many visitors who had flocked to the city to enjoy the social amenities presided over by Beau Nash earlier in the eighteenth century, magnificent new squares, terraces and crescents had been built with stone quarried locally at Coombe Down, a softly-glowing, honey-coloured limestone. These spread up the hill slopes to the north of the small medieval city confined within a loop of the Avon, and over the river to the east. The city itself was transformed but the beautiful abbey, rebuilt in the fifteenth century, and the layout of the narrow streets that link their arms around it, serve as reminders of Bath's two thousand years of history. The Georgian town planners, however, were not interested in Bath's Roman remains nor its medieval past and built their new city on top of the old. Today, Bath is still a wonderful Georgian city. To walk round its streets and into the hills that surround the city in Jane's own footsteps and those of her characters is an unforgettable experience. We are really walking in her world.

As well as *Northanger Abbey* Jane set part of her last complete novel, *Persuasion*, in Bath. Although she seldom describes the city — she could safely assume her readers were as familiar with its appearance as she was — she captures its

View of Bath from Beechen Cliff

special atmosphere through her characters' reactions and the skilful use of accurate and precise detail. So clever a novelist was she, that as we walk it seems almost inevitable that we should pass Anne Elliot and Captain Wentworth in Milsom Street or encounter Catherine Morland with the Tilneys on the top of Beechen Cliff.

Our first walk in Bath is about five miles round. We start close to Number 1 Paragon, where Jane stayed during her earliest visits to the city. If you arrive by car, park at the bottom of Walcot Street in the large car park. From the park, turn right to walk up Walcot Street until you come to a flight of steps on the left. The steps lead you up to the Paragon, a curving terrace of tall eighteenth-century houses with pediments over windows and doorways, and wrought-iron balconies and railings. Number 1 is the first house on your right. Jane came to visit her uncle and aunt Leigh Perrot. Uncle James was her mother's brother. (She had been a Miss Leigh, resident in Bath before her marriage.) Upon inheriting some property he had added his extra surname. He suffered from attacks of gout and spent part of every year in Bath. In a letter to Cassandra, written from Bath in 1799, Jane recalls a previous visit in November 1797. But we can imagine her here, even earlier, at the age of nineteen as, in a letter dated 1801 in which she describes watching a display of horsemanship at the Bath riding school, she mentions a display she watched some seven years previously. No doubt she enjoyed the dancing, parties and social life as much as her heroine Catherine, but, as her satirical portrait of the shallow flirt Isabella proves, her sharp eyes were as always quick to discover a person's true value; no amount of fine clothes or show of manners could conceal from her the evils she disliked most — selfishness and greed.

We can imagine Jane arriving at the Paragon; stepping out of the coach on to the wide raised pavements — properly paved, cleaned and lit from the 'reign' of Beau Nash — to be welcomed by Frank, the manservant, then greeted by her aunt and uncle, anxiously enquiring about her mother's

Edgar's Buildings, Bath

The archway leading from the Abbey churchyard into Cheap Street, Bath

health and eager for news of her sailor brothers. They would
refer to the newspaper to give her news about Bath and the
names of the latest arrivals and perhaps her uncle would tell
her about any interesting folk he had met that morning in
the Pump Room while taking his regulation three glasses of
water. Fashionable life in Bath was well regulated. As Catherine Morland finds, 'Every morning now brought its regular
duties: shops to be visited; some new part of the town to be
looked at; and the Pump Room to be attended.' But as the
numerous 'walks', 'promenades' and 'parades' in Bath suggest,
the paramount concern of all was to walk about as elegantly
dressed as possible, to see and to be seen. We will follow Jane
as she accompanies her uncle on his 'morning circuit'.

From Number 1 Paragon, turn left, then cross the top of
Broad Street into George Street. On the right, facing down
fashionable Milsom Street is Edgar's Buildings where, in
Northanger Abbey, Isabella was in lodgings with her family
to be visited by her unlikeable brother John. Jane cleverly
chooses locations in Bath to suit her characters. From such a
vantage spot, Isabella could watch for handsome young men —
when not immersed in one of her favourite 'horrid' romances
of course! Follow the raised pavement to the end of George
Street, then turn left down Gay Street. Ahead you have a
splendid view of Beechen Cliff, still, as Jane describes it,
'that noble hill whose beautiful verdure and hanging coppice
render it so striking an object from almost every opening in
Bath'. Soon you come to Queen's Square, John Wood the
elder's masterpiece, on your right. The north side of the
square is complete, built in the heavier early Georgian style
with Corinthian columns surmounted by a massive pediment.
Walk to the corner of the southern side of the square. Here,
at Number 13, Jane and her mother spent a midsummer
holiday in 1799 with Edward, his wife Elizabeth, and their
two elder children. Jane writes to Cassandra that they are
all very comfortable, and that 'a little black kitten runs about
the staircase'. She looks out of the drawing room window as
she writes to tell her sister that the view 'is far more cheerful,

than Paragon'. In later letters she tells of shopping expeditions to buy stockings for Anna, shoes for Martha (she has
doubts about the fit) and a lace-trimmed cloak for herself.
The latest fashion she says is to trim your hat with artificial
fruit, and comments, 'I cannot help thinking, it is more
natural to have flowers grow out of your head than fruit'.
We remember Mrs Croft in *Persuasion*, 'tied by the heel' with
a blister through devotedly accompanying her husband
ordered to walk for his health, when Jane writes that her
uncle has 'over-walked himself and can now only travel in
a chair'.

While Edward drinks the waters and bathes, Jane enjoys
some country walks, attends a firework display in Sydney
Gardens and mingles with the fashionable crowd in the Royal
Crescent to watch Lady Willoughby 'present the Colours to
some Corps of Yeomanry or other'.

Turn left down Prince's Street, then take the first left
turning along Beaufort Square. Cross the road and walk
straight ahead down Trim Street, once the home of Sheridan.
You are now in the heart of the charming narrow ways
clustered around the abbey, Georgian in design with their
colourful shops with bow windows and classical doorways,
but quite medieval in their shape. Turn right at the end of
Trim Street, then left to walk along Upper Boro' Walls until
you come to Union Passage on the right. This most delightful
of narrow footways, crowded with fascinating shops, was the
only thoroughfare to Cheap Street at the time of Jane's
earlier visits to Bath. Shopping must have had its perilous
moments when these narrow ways became blocked with
horses and carriages and sedan chairs. Follow Union Passage
to cross Cheap Street. Although the traffic may be different
today, it is no more difficult to cross than it was when
Isabella, with the puzzled Catherine in tow, was halted in
her pursuit of 'the odious' young men she had noticed eyeing
her in the Pump Room. Go under the arch into the paved
square in front of the abbey, still called the Churchyard.

Ahead of you is the Pump Room. Here everyone met to

The Pump Room, Bath

Print: Interior of the Pump Room, Bath, 1805. Aquatint engraving by J. C. Nattes

take the waters, exchange news and gossip, and review the latest fashions. The atmosphere of the room, with its soft pale blue, cream and gold colouring is harmonious and restful. As you collected your glass of water from the steaming fountain in the centre of the long wall, musicians played in the gallery in the semicircular alcove at one end of the room. In the opposite alcove, a bust of Beau Nash stands above the clock beneath which Mrs Allen renewed her acquaintance with Mrs Thorpe, while noticing that 'the lace on Mrs Thorpe's pelisse was not half so handsome as that on her own'.

Like all visitors, Jane will have attended services at the abbey. The light streaming through the abbey's great perpendicular windows has given this lovely building the name, 'The lantern of the West'. Pass the abbey on your right and walk round the Orange Grove to the balustrades lining the Grand Parade, overlooking the gardens sloping down to the river. This was the site of the Lower Assembly Rooms where, at a ball, Catherine is introduced to the 'all-conquering' Henry Tilney by the Master of Ceremonies, Mr. King. (He was a real person, presiding over the Lower Rooms until 1805.) Turn right and follow the Grand Parade into Pierrepont Street. Now look for two solid columns either side of a small arch on the right. Go through the arch into Old Orchard Street. Follow this old cobbled alley as it bears left to the Masonic Hall, the site of the former theatre. This was the theatre which Jane attended. It was the first theatre outside London to be granted a Royal patent and here Sarah Siddons became famous. (She was a neighbour of the Leigh Perrots in the Paragon.)

Turn left along Henry Street, then left again down Pierrepont Street. Now turn right to follow North Parade to the bridge. Go into the second small tower you see on the left-hand side of the bridge and down the spiral staircase to the footpath beside the Avon. We are now following the route Catherine and the Tilneys took to the top of Beechen Cliff. Turn left and follow the river, under the railway. Cross Claverton Road and follow the sign for Lyncombe Hill.

Turn right into Calton Road and you will see a steep flight of steps on the left. Climb the steps as they take you to the top of Beechen Cliff. Our way bears right at the top, under the spreading boughs of great beech trees to give a wonderful view of Bath, far below in the valley framed by rounded hillsides. To the right, the village of Widcombe where Jane walked with her acquaintance Mrs Chamberlayne is hidden in the fold of a deep valley. Looking down at Bath from the top of the cliff one can almost overhear Henry Tilney instructing Catherine on the art of the picturesque with such good effect that 'when they gained the top of Beechen Cliff she voluntarily rejected the whole city of Bath as unworthy to make part of a landscape'.

Follow the path as it leads over the hilltop until you come to a flight of steps on the right. These quickly bring you down to a lane through a housing estate. Bear right down the lane and take the path on the left to a subway which takes you under the road and railway to the river. Cross the bridge. Walk up Southgate into Stall Street. Now go under the archway on the right into Abbey Square, a charming spot with its old inn and enormous plane tree. Walk on to York Street, then turn left into Stall Street again. Go right now to pass the colonnades in front of the abbey churchyard. On the left is the site of the White Hart, the most important of Bath's coaching inns. It was here that Jane set the scene for the Musgrove family's visit in *Persuasion* where, in the crowded general sitting room, Captain Wentworth overhears his gentle Anne defend the constancy of woman's love.

Cross Cheap Street and keep straight on up Union Street and Old Bond Street to Bath's most famous thoroughfare, Milsom Street. Now we are surrounded by Jane's characters! Catherine Morland runs frequently up and down Milsom Street to visit the Tilneys who have their lodgings here and to call on the Thorpes. In *Persuasion* Anne Elliot encounters her genial acquaintance, Admiral Croft, as he stands, laughing heartily, outside a print shop window. 'I can never get by this shop without stopping,' he tells her, 'what queer fellows your fine painters must be, to think that anybody would venture their lives in such a shapeless old cockleshell as that . . . I would not venture over a horsepond in it.' Number 2, Milsom Street, was Mollands the pastry cooks where Anne took shelter from the rain, to be offered the use of his umbrella by Captain Wentworth who had, as he claims, equipped himself properly for Bath.

Cross to the right of Edgar's Buildings to walk up Bartlett Street. Turn left along Alfred Street, then right to the main entrance to the Upper Rooms. Jane danced in the great green and gold ballroom, designed by John Wood the younger,

The Upper Rooms, Bath

beneath the sparkle of its five magnificent crystal chandeliers while musicians played in their gracefully curved balcony. Poor Catherine, chaperoned by Mrs Allen, is only just able to squeeze inside at the height of the season. Even when, with enormous effort, they gain the top of the room, all they are able to see are the tall feathers of some of the ladies' head-dresses. In the larger of the octagon rooms, gentlemen could gamble away their fortunes and even the sensible Mr Allen is tempted to try a mild flutter. You can also see the elegant concert room (or tea room on ball nights) where Anne came to realise with a mixture of pain and pleasure that Captain Wentworth was jealous of the attentions her cousin, William Walter Elliot, was paying her.

Turn right into Bennett Street, then left to climb Belvedere. When the road divides, turn right into Camden Crescent. This magnificent terrace, standing high above the city, is just the place you would expect Anne's father, the vain Sir Walter Elliot, to choose as his residence. It is indeed as Jane says, 'a lofty, dignified situation, such as becomes a man of consequence'. Now you look south over Bath towards Beechen Cliff. Walk back to Belvedere, but at the end of Camden Crescent, turn left down a lane. Go right down some steps towards Hedgemead Gardens. Just past a turning on the right you come to an iron gate. Go right, through the gate into the gardens and follow the path across this pleasant hillside park. Below you will see Walcot church where Jane's parents were married, and her father is buried. Steps in front of the church bring you down to a lane. Turn right to walk back to the Paragon, then left to return to the steps by Number 1. Go down the steps into Walcot Street and turn right for the car park.

All information about Bath – including where to stay – can be obtained from an excellent Information Bureau in the Abbey Churchyard. A combined ticket can be obtained for guided tours of the **Pump Room** and **Roman Baths** and **Upper Rooms**. A splendid collection of costumes is housed in the Upper Rooms.

Map 6

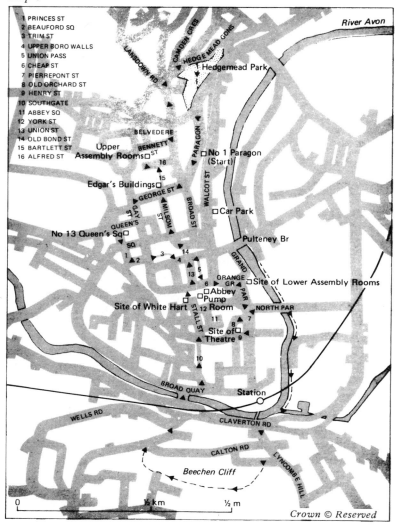

1	PRINCES ST
2	BEAUFORD SQ
3	TRIM ST
4	UPPER BORO WALLS
5	UNION PASS
6	CHEAP ST
7	PIERREPONT ST
8	OLD ORCHARD ST
9	HENRY ST
10	SOUTHGATE
11	ABBEY SQ
12	YORK ST
13	UNION ST
14	OLD BOND ST
15	BARTLETT ST
16	ALFRED ST

River Avon

Hedgemead Park

LANSDOWN RD · CAMDEN CRES · HEDGE MEAD GDNS · PARAGON · WALCOT ST

BELVEDERE · BENNETT ST

Upper Assembly Rooms □ ST

□ No 1 Paragon (Start)

Edgar's Buildings □

GEORGE ST · GAY ST · MILSOM ST · BROAD ST · QUEEN'S SQ

No 13 Queen's Sq □

□ Car Park

Pulteney Br

GRAND PAR · ORANGE GR

□ Site of Lower Assembly Rooms

□ Abbey Pump Room

Site of White Hart

STALL ST · NORTH PAR

Site of Theatre

BROAD QUAY

Station

WELLS RD · CLAVERTON RD

CALTON RD · LYNCOMBE HILL

Beechen Cliff

0 ········· ½ km ········· ½ m

Crown © Reserved

Key   ▶ Route of Walk   – – – – – – Footpaths and bridleways

Park off Walcot Street. Walk up Walcot Street to steps on left. Climb these to the Paragon. Turn left down Paragon, cross Broad Street into George Street. Left down Gay Street to Queen's Square. Walk right to Number 13, left down Prince's Street, left into Beaufort Square. Cross road, down Trim Street, through arch on right then left along Upper Boro' Walls and right down Union Passage. Cross Cheap Street, through arch into Abbey Churchyard. Abbey on right, walk round Orange Grove to Grand Parade. Turn right into Pierrepont Street, then right through arch into Old Orchard Street. Left along Henry Street, left down Pierrepont Street, then right down North Parade to the Bridge. Go into second little tower on left and down spiral staircase to footpath by the river. Turn left and follow the river bank, under railway to Claverton Road. Cross and follow signs for Lyncombe Hill. Turn right into Calton Road, then climb steps on left to top of Beechen Cliff. Walk along cliff to steps leading down on right. Turn right to walk back to main road, then turn left under the railway and over the river bridge. Walk up Southgate into Stall Street, under archway on right into Abbey Square. On to York Street, left to Stall Street and turn right to cross Cheap Street. Straight on up Union Street, Old Bond Street, Milsom Street. Cross to the right of Edgar's Buildings up Bartlett Street. Turn left along Alfred Street, then right past Upper Rooms. . Turn right into Bennett Street, then left up Belvedere, to bear right for Camden Crescent. Where Camden Crescent joins Belvedere, follow lane on left towards Hedgemead Gardens. Go through gate on right and across the Gardens to descend steps to the road. Turn right for the Paragon, left to Number 1 to descend the steps to Walcot Street. Right for car park.

Distance: about five miles. Some steep climbs and a great deal to see so I would recommend a full day for this tour.

7

Residence in Bath

There is a whole world of difference between visiting a place for a holiday and actually making a home there as I am sure Jane felt when, after a visit to Ibthorpe in November 1800, shortly before her twenty-fifth birthday, she returned to Steventon with Martha to be greeted by her mother's announcement: 'Well girls! It is all settled. We have decided to leave Steventon and go to Bath.' Tradition records that Jane fainted. But she quickly reconciled herself to the move. Although she must leave the country life she loved, there were some advantages: her brother James would be able to take over the Steventon living, neither of her parents enjoyed good health and they already knew Bath well and had a wide circle of friends and acquaintances there. Bath itself was changing. Although still popular with invalids, it was no longer the glittering magnet to the wealthy and fashionable that it had been during the eighteenth century. They were being tempted away by seaside resorts like Brighton. People were going to Bath to settle, not to hire lodgings for the season. It was becoming more a place to retire to than elope from. The great Assembly Rooms were thinly attended as people preferred to give private parties in their own homes. In *Persuasion*, written thirteen years after *Northanger Abbey*, Jane reflects these social changes.

Her own attitude towards Bath is possibly different also. The heroine of *Persuasion*, Anne Elliot, is a much more sedate character than Catherine Morland. She has suffered from a heart-breaking love affair and receives no comfort from her family. After the quiet of her country home she finds 'the white glare' of Bath exhausting and persists 'in a very determined, though very silent, disinclination' for the city. Although Jane is not Anne, she could be voicing her own views here after six years' residence in Bath: years in which she suffered from considerable emotional and physical stress. But Jane does not undervalue the attraction of Bath. Anne's friend, the sensible Lady Russell, returns to the city with delight: 'When Lady Russell was entering Bath on a wet afternoon, and driving through the long course of streets from the Old Bridge to Camden Place, amidst the dash of other carriages, the heavy rumble of carts and drays, the bawling of newsmen, muffin-men and milkmen, and the ceaseless clink of pattens, she made no complaint. No, these were noises which belonged to the winter pleasures; her spirits rose under their influence.'

The Leigh Perrots invited the Austen family to stay with them in the Paragon while they hunted for a suitable house. On Tuesday, 5 May 1801, Jane writes to Cassandra (who is at Ibthorpe helping to nurse the sick Mrs Lloyd) that they have arrived safely. Although she has only been in Bath a few hours, she had noticed that, apart from fish, food is cheaper. The following week she tells Cassandra all about the last ball of the season, held in the Upper Rooms, which she attends. The mood she was to portray in *Persuasion* is foreshadowed in her comments: 'Before tea, it was rather a dull affair . . . think of four couples, surrounded by about an hundred people, dancing in the Upper Rooms at Bath! After tea we *cheered up*, the breaking up of private parties sent some more scores to the Ball.' Jane's reaction to people is as sharp as ever. She tells Cassandra that she had no difficulty in picking out the mistress of a certain Mr Evelyn from among the crowd. 'I have a very good eye at an adulteress . . . she looked rather quietly and contentedly silly than anything else.' But, she adds, Mr Evelyn seems harmless enough, 'he gets groundsel for his birds and all that' and Jane accepts a drive with him in his 'handsome phaeton and four' up Landsdown Hill.

After Cassandra joined the family in Bath, there are no more letters from Jane until September 1804. Even if Cassandra had received any it is likely she would have destroyed them as too personal. For during the summer of 1801 while on holiday by the sea, Jane met a young clergyman whom she might have married. Instead of rejoining her as he promised, she received a message to say he was dead.

Jane had little time to indulge in sorrow. By the end of the year the Austens had rented their own house, 4 Sydney Place, at the eastern end of Pulteney Street, facing the Sydney Gardens. Her father was now experiencing frequent bouts of illness and her mother became gravely ill also. That Jane and Cassandra were devoted nurses is proved by some verses Mrs Austen wrote upon her recovery which she attributed in part 'to the care of my daughters whom heaven will bless'. We can be sure that Jane sought some relaxation in the walks in Sydney Gardens, along the Avon valley and by the canal, and to the villages in the hills around Bath which she describes in earlier letters. This walk, about seven miles round, follows her on some of her rambles.

If you arrive by car, park at the bottom of Walcot Street in the large car park. Walk across Pulteney Bridge into Laura Place where, in *Persuasion*, Lady Dalrymple and her daughter were 'living in style'. Turn left into Henrietta Street. A few yards down this road on the right you will see an archway leading into Henrietta Mews. Walk through and on down the Mews, with Henrietta Park on your left till you come to some steps on the right. Climb these into Pulteney Street. Turn left to walk down this beautiful wide street of classically elegant terraces built by Thomas Baldwin in the style of Robert Adam. Here, in *Northanger Abbey*, Catherine Morland and the Allens had lodgings. We can imagine her anxious face behind a window, watching the rain and wondering if Henry Tilney and his sister will call to take her on the promised country walk. Who could forget Mrs Allen's reassuring words?

She 'had no doubt in the world of its being a very fine day, if the clouds would only go off, and the sun keep out'.

Turn left into Sydney Place and walk round to Number 4. It is a simple terrace house, not as grand as those in Pulteney Street but with a pleasant outlook over the Gardens. Jane lived here for three years. During this time she attempted some writing: revising *Susan* (later to be called *Northanger Abbey*) which she sold to Crosby for £10 in 1803. Crosby advertised the novel, but did not publish it. However, the sale may have encouraged Jane to start a new novel, *The Watsons*, which is written on paper with a Bath watermark. But after writing 17,500 words she abandoned the story and it was never finished.

Pulteney Bridge, Bath

'Yesterday was a busy day with me,' Jane wrote to Cassandra. 'I was walking almost all day long; I went to Sydney Gardens soon after one, and did not return till four.' Cross the road in front of the house as Jane did, to the building which is now the Holburne of Menstrie Museum at the entrance to the Gardens. In Jane's time this was a hotel, Sydney House or Tavern, with a ball room, tea and card rooms, a coffee room, and a taproom for coach drivers and chair-men in the cellar. The museum is famous for its collection of furniture, porcelain, glass and paintings. With the museum on your left walk a few yards up the Sydney Road to enter the Gardens through a gate on the left. Bear right over the sloping lawns towards a row of stone balusters which run along the top of the most elegant of railway embankments. Walk towards the little pavilion, built in the classical

The Canal near Bathampton

style with columns, a little to your left. This reminded me of the former glories of this now quiet park. As popular pleasure grounds they were Bath's equivalent to London's Vauxhall or Ranelagh. There was a maze which Jane mentions in a letter, public breakfasts, and gala nights with music and fireworks. Bear right over the railway bridge towards a large house. Now you cross another bridge, this time over the Kennet and Avon Canal. Our walk continues in Jane's footsteps along the canal towpath.

Walk straight on through the park, leaving the large house on your left. Go up some steps to the Sydney Road. Turn left, then left again into Beckford Road. Cross the road and walk for a few yards down the hill until you come to a footpath on the right leading to the canal towpath. Follow this past the lock-keeper's cottage. Suddenly you have left the busy street behind to enter a leafy world of meadowsweet and moorhens. The only sounds are the rustle of the reeds trailing in the water and the flop of the occasional fish as it breaks the surface. Follow the towpath to Bathampton. Just before Bathampton bridge, leave the canal to turn left down some steps to the road beside the George Inn. On the right is the church of St Nicholas, famous as the burial place of Admiral Arthur Phillip who led the first settlers to Australia and became the first governor of New South Wales. Like Mr Austen, he decided to retire to Bath. Jane would not have to look far in Bath for inspiration for Admiral Croft. Follow the road ahead over the railway, past Bathampton Manor, to cross the Avon by a magnificent toll bridge, 102 years old. Just over the bridge, turn left following the public footpath sign into the meadows beside the river. The path runs towards the river for a few yards, then bears right towards the corner of a hedge. With the hedge on your right at first, follow the path over the meadows. It is a lovely walk. The river runs beneath its fringe of willows beside us, and our way leads through spinneys full of the chatter of birds and wild flowers. Keep straight on beside the river under the bypass bridges along a tarmac lane, then keep ahead along a tree-shaded footpath to the main road, the A4.

Turn left to walk down to the traffic lights, then turn right up Gloucester Road. In about half a mile you pass the former Bladud Arms on the left. Now turn left down Ferndale Road, bear left for a few yards, then cross the road and turn right up Valley View Road. When the road divides, bear right, up the hill, then right again at the next division. We are now back in country lanes. Charlcombe Lane joins our way from the left. Keep straight on and when the road divides, bear left round the top of a valley towards Charlcombe. Sheltered within the hills, Charlcombe is still the delightful old world village that Jane discovered when she walked here one June evening in 1799. She writes: 'We took a very charming walk from 6 to 8 up Beacon Hill, and across some fields to the village of Charlcombe, which is sweetly situated in a little green valley, as a village with such a name ought to be.' As you pass the last stone house of the village, almost at the other side of the valley, look very carefully for a lane on your right with a church notice board. Follow this a few steps to the church of St Mary the Virgin. I believe this must be the smallest, but one of the most delightful Norman churches in England. I am sure Jane must have come to this church, still as in her day, framed by green hillsides where children gather wild flowers. For here, Henry Fielding, the author of *Tom Jones*, a novelist Jane admired in spite of what she called his 'low standard of morals', was married. Tradition maintains that St Mary the Virgin is the Mother Church of Bath and that Bath Abbey used to pay its dues of a pound of peppercorns annually.

Retrace your steps and follow Charlcombe Lane as it curves left round the valley. Pass two flights of stone steps on the right and just past a house named 'Carmel' climb another flight of steps on the right to walk up steep Van Dieman's Lane to the Landsdown Road. Turn right for a few yards, then cross over to follow Fonthill Road which leads to three possible tracks. Bear left over a stile to a grassy hillside, Primrose Hill. Like Jane, you will enjoy a splendid view. Bear half-left diagonally down the hillside then turn right with a hedge on your left. After about fifty yards turn left over a stile.

The view from Charlcombe

Charlcombe Church

Now keep ahead down the field crossing more stiles and fields to meet a wide crosstrack. Turn left and follow the track which becomes a narrow path leading straight ahead uphill past Primrose Hill Farm which will be on your left. Follow the path and cross the road to climb the steps into Summerhill Road. Keep to the right of Summerhill Road, to turn right down Sion Hill – a favourite walk of Jane's. The road bears left to bring you to a chestnut-shaded path leading over the golf course. Follow this to Weston Road, opposite Royal Victoria Park. Turn left to the crossroads, then right to walk past Marlborough Buildings, the home in *Persuasion* of Colonel Wallis and his pretty wife we hear so much about.

Now you turn left into Royal Crescent, designed by John Wood the Younger. This is a magnificent curving terrace of thirty houses designed as one harmonious whole with rows of Ionic columns supporting a continuous frieze. The Crescent,

The Circus, Bath

with its wide pavements and cobbled carriageway, overlooking fields sloping down to the Avon, was a favourite promenade for the citizens of Bath. Jane writes often of walking here, as do her characters. Number 1, still equipped with its iron torch snuffer on the railings by the door, is open to the public. Inside the rooms are furnished with typical eighteenth century elegance. The kitchen which contains a display of weight-driven spits in action is particularly fascinating. Walk down Brock Street to the Circus. This beautiful circle of sweeping terraces was the work of both the Woods. It is exciting to stand there, enclosed by the eighteenth century!

From the Circus, turn right down Gay Street. At Number 25 Jane and her mother lived quietly for a few months in 1805. Turn right to walk round Queen's Square, then right again down Chapel Row. Go straight on down Charles Street to Green Park Buildings, a dignified terrace still, facing part of what was once the famous Kingsmead fields, the scene of duels. In 1804, the Austens left Sydney Place for Number 27, Green Park Buildings. It is a pleasant house with delicate fan tracery over the door. Perhaps they moved so that Mr Austen could be nearer the Pump Room as he was growing daily more infirm. The end came suddenly. In January 1805 Jane writes to her brother Frank that her father is dead. There can be no doubt of the grief in these two moving letters. 'His tenderness as a father, who can do justice to?' she writes. After the short stay in Gay Street, the bereaved family made one more move in Bath, to Trim Street, early in 1806, before leaving the city in June.

Before we leave Bath, we must visit the Guildhall to see another lovely room Jane probably knew. Turn right down James' Street, then left in Kingsmead Square. Walk along Westgate Street and Cheap Street to cross the High Street to the Guildhall. Inside you must see the Banqueting Hall, a beautiful room inspired by the designs of Robert Adam. The room is still used for important public occasions as it was in Jane's time. From the Guildhall walk up the High Street and the car park where we began our walk is on your right.

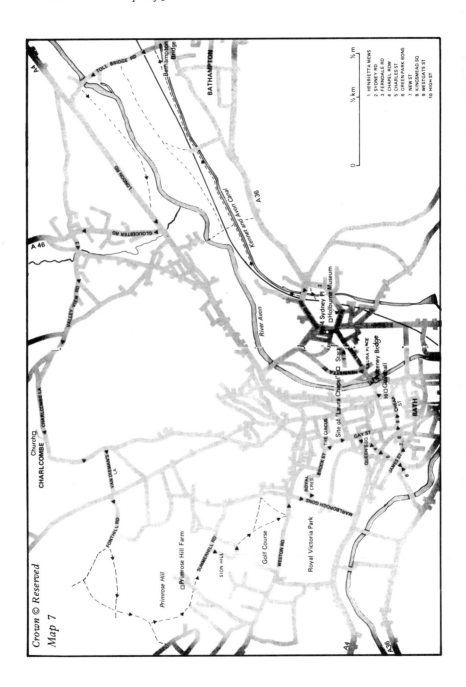

Map 7

Key   ► Route of Walk   _ _ _ _ _ _ Footpaths and bridleways

Park off Walcot Street. Cross Pulteney Bridge into Laura Place. Turn left down Henrietta Street for a few yards, then right through arch into Henrietta Mews. Walk down Mews (Henrietta Park on your left), turn right up steps into Pulteney Street. Left down Pulteney Street, left into Sydney Place. Cross road to Holburne of Menstrie Museum, then with Museum on your left walk up Sydney Road for a few yards to gate into Sydney Gardens. Bear right over gardens, over railway, over canal, to pass large house on left. Up steps to Sydney Road. Left, then left again into Beckford Road. Right down footpath to canal towpath. Follow canal to Bathampton. Just before bridge, turn left to road by George Inn. Keep straight on over toll-bridge, then follow public footpath sign right into meadows by river. Make for hedge. With hedge on right at first, follow path over meadows then beside river, under bypass bridges to A4, London Road. Turn left to lights, then right up Gloucester Road to former Bladud Arms. Turn left down Ferndale Road, left for a few yards, then right up Valley View Road. Road divides, bear right, then right again at next division. Keep straight on following the road as it bears left for Charlcombe village. Follow footpath sign on right to see church and return to the road to continue along road as it bears left around the valley. Pass two flights of steps on the right and just past house named 'Carmel' turn right up steps to climb steep Van Dieman's Lane. Turn right for a few yards then cross road to follow Fonthill Road. At the end, three possible ways, bear left over stile to Primrose Hill. Walk half-left down the hillside. At foot turn right, hedge on left and continue for about 50 yards. Turn left over stile and keep ahead downhill over stiles and fields to a good crosstrack. Turn left along track which becomes a narrow path past Primrose Hill Farm (on your left). Cross road, climb steps into Summerhill Road. Keep to right of Summerhill Road, then turn right down Sion Hill Road. Road bears left, turn right down footpath over golf course to Weston Road. Turn left to junctions, then right past Marlborough Buildings. Left past Royal Crescent, down Brock Street to the Circus. Right down Gay Street, right round Queen's Square, right down Chapel Row, straight on down Charles Street to Green Park Buildings. Right down James Street, then left to Kingsmead Square. Bear right along Westgate Street, Cheap Street to cross High Street to Guildhall. Straight up High Street to car park on right.
Distance: about seven miles. Some steep climbs – allow a full day.

8

Holidays in Devon

In the summer of 1801 Jane and Cassandra accompanied their parents to Sidmouth and the following summer they were again in Devon, staying in Dawlish and Teignmouth. The long wars with Napoleon had restricted foreign travel and these quiet resorts were quickly becoming fashionable watering places. It was probably at this time, when she was twenty-six, that Jane experienced her most serious love affair. Just how serious this was is difficult to tell as all the real information we have about it is a few tantalising hints dropped by Cassandra many years later. Mrs Bellas, Anna's daughter, wrote that Cassandra referred to Jane meeting a gentleman 'whose charm of person, mind and manners was such that she thought him worthy to possess and likely to win her sister's love'. They parted, after arranging to meet later in their holiday. But Jane never saw him again; he died a few weeks afterwards.

Jane's letters convey no hint of the affair as Cassandra destroyed the more personal of her sister's correspondence as she did her own. But it seems likely that this was indeed a serious attachment, that Jane suffered a great deal and as she could not withdraw from society had to control and conceal her feelings. This kind of suffering and the need to control strong emotions is the central theme of *Sense and Sensibility* published in 1811. Although the first draft of the novel — then called *Elinor and Marianne* — was written at

Steventon Jane revised the early manuscript as soon as she had a settled home again at Chawton in 1809. I am sure that as a result of her own experience Jane was able to portray with far greater perception the sufferings of Marianne, spurned by the man to whom she had given her heart, and Elinor, who has not only lost the man she loves but is also compelled to listen to the confidences of the girl who has won him. A story which possibly began as a fairly straight-forward contrast between the two sisters and the way they behaved in similar circumstances became, I believe, a far more complex study of character in the final version. Although Elinor is shown behaving correctly at all times, controlling her feelings, preserving the social forms and supporting her sister, it is the impulsive Marianne — who gives way to every emotion and conceals nothing — who somehow appears the more attractive character. It is as if Jane's head is with Elinor — the demands of society must be met — but her heart is with Marianne. The significance of this extensive revision is suggested I believe by the fact that Jane sets much of the novel in Devon, in the 'Barton Valley', in and around 'Barton Park' which the novel tells us is 'within four miles northward of Exeter'. This beautiful part of the Exe valley would have been a reasonable journey for her to have made from the coast during one of her Devon holidays.

The Devon setting of the novel is also important for its own sake. In *Sense and Sensibility* as in *Mansfield Park* Jane draws a strong contrast between the values and standards of the country and those of the town. The Dashwood family who have passed most of their time in the country are shown as kind, honest and industrious. Although they are deceived by the heartless town-bred Steeles and the worldly Willoughby, they finally win for themselves a secure and reasonably happy future. But, as in *Mansfield Park* country life also brings its dangers. Idleness and wealth produce the insipid Lady Middleton of Barton Park: lack of knowledge of the world has potentially disastrous consequences for both

Marianne Dashwood and Edward Ferrars.

Although there is no written evidence to support my belief I have planned this walk to explore what I think is the part of the Exe valley which Jane calls 'Barton' in *Sense and Sensibility*. (Barton is so common among Devon place-names that it is not surprising Jane should choose it for the name of the valley, the large house and cottage and nearby village in her novel.) Jane always wrote about places she knew, and she must have had a specific large estate in mind. I feel sure her 'Barton Park' is Pynes, still, as in the novel, a 'large and handsome house'. Then, as now, it was the home of the Northcote family. The Dowager Countess of Iddesleigh (a title taken by the Northcotes) told me that traditionally Pynes has always been linked with the novel and her view was confirmed by other local people. It seems likely that Jane and her family, while they were on holiday in Devon, were invited to visit there. They would probably have stayed at Pynes several days and Jane would have had time to enjoy some of the beautiful country walks that are undertaken by the equally energetic Elinor and Marianne in the novel. The village of 'Barton', on the hillside, close to Barton Park, corresponds exactly with Upton Pyne. It is more difficult to place 'Barton Cottage' which we are told is about half a mile from Barton Park. No site seemed to me to fit all the clues given in the novel. However, as I explored the area, I con-cluded that Jane possibly imagined the cottage to be near the farm at Woodrow Barton — a suggestion that was first made to me by Mrs. E. M. Cornall who lives locally. Our walk is about three miles round with breathtaking views all the way.

We start in the centre of Upton Pyne, in the tiny cobbled square where there is room to park in front of the church. If you follow the A396 due north from Exeter you will approach the Barton Valley from the same direction as the Dashwoods in the novel. After about three miles the Exe is joined by the Creedy. Turn left along the A377 over the bridge to follow the Crediton road for little over quarter of a mile. Turn right following the sign to Upton Pyne. The lane takes you over

Old cottages at Upton Pyne

the Creedy then turns left to wind uphill to the village. Drive through the village, over the crest of the hill and look for the tower of Upton Pyne church on the hillside a little to your left. The turning into the square in front of the church is on your left but it is narrow and easily missed. It is immediately opposite a stone obelisk memorial and you turn between a high hedge and the wall of a whitewashed cob-and-thatch cottage.

Now you are standing in the midst of a scene that can scarcely have changed at all with the centuries. Across the cobbles ahead an old lych gate admits you to the churchyard and a cluster of thatched cottages, deep-eaved and tranquil, enclose the square on the opposite side. Here, in the church of St Mary, Elinor Dashwood and Edward Ferrars were married. The church is built of local volcanic stone and has a particularly lovely tower. On each corner of the tower is carved the figure of an Evangelist and over the door there is

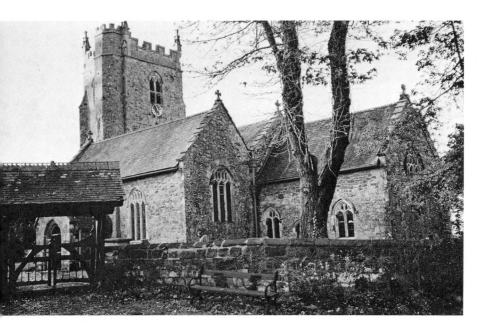

Upton Pyne church and churchyard

a figure of Christ so placed as to appear to be blessing the people as they enter. The church stands high and from it there is a magnificent view over lush valleys and low rolling downs to the steep slopes of the Raddon Hills. No wonder Marianne Dashwood responded with so much enthusiastic delight to so much beauty! And even the more prosaic Edward, although he cannot join her in such raptures over 'the picturesque', enjoys his rambles to the village while he is staying at Barton Cottage: 'Edward returned to them with fresh admiration of the surrounding country; in his walk to the village, he had seen many parts of the valley to advantage; and the village itself, in a much higher situation than the cottage, afforded a general view of the whole which had exceedingly pleased him'. We will follow him back to Barton Cottage.

Return to the lane from the square and turn right to walk back through the village. After a short distance you will come to a lane on the left signposted Brampford Speke. Turn left and follow this with woods on your right and a wonderful view of Upton Pyne and the valleys beyond over the low green bank on your left. After about a quarter of a mile we leave the lane to turn right along a bridleway, possibly unsigned, between the edge of the woods and the fields. So turn right past a gateway when the woods end to follow the good track with the trees at first on your right. Wide views of the Exe valley open in front of you. Much as they missed their former country home at Norland, the Dashwoods were cheered by their first sight of this lovely valley. They saw it as we do today: 'a pleasant, fertile spot, well-wooded and rich in pasture'. The track drops fairly steeply downhill. It was while running down these hills that I believe Marianne fell and twisted her foot. She was carried home by Willoughby and so the introduction was made that was to affect her future life so much. After passing through the farmyard at Woodrow Barton, the track turns right. Follow it round and now on your right are some cottages that remind me very much of Jane's description of Barton Cottage and it is here that I imagine the home of the Dashwoods. The houses stand well, fairly high on the hillside, with exactly the view that the Dashwoods enjoy from their front windows: 'It commanded the whole of the valley, and reached into the country beyond. The hills which surrounded the cottage terminated the valley in that direction; under another name, and in another course, it branched out again between two of the steepest of them'. (The second valley which sheltered Willoughby's home at 'Allenham' is I believe the valley of the Creedy and the village which corresponds with the description in the novel is Newton St Cyres. We will call there later.)

Woodrow Barton is correctly placed about a quarter of a mile from Pynes, and the Dashwoods could walk through the park to visit the Middletons without any inconvenience. As in the novel, the Dashwoods would pass close to Pynes to arrive at the cottage but once there, they would find the mansion: 'screened from their view at home by the projection of an hill'. But in the story it is possible to see Barton village from the cottage windows. Even without the woods this would be difficult today, but it is quite likely that the village was more extensive in the eighteenth century. I also have a suspicion that the hills gained in height in Jane's memory! However, Elinor and Marianne walk one day from the cottage 'along the road through the valley . . . beyond the entrance to the valley, where the country, though still rich, was less wild and more open'. They then see 'a long stretch of the road which they had travelled on first coming to Barton'. This describes exactly the point where the Creedy joins the Exe and they could be looking towards Exeter. As this is 'a prospect which formed the distance of their view from the cottage' it seems very likely that Jane had somewhere around Woodrow Barton in mind as their home. She tells us that the front gate of the cottage opened immediately off the route followed by the Dashwoods when they arrived. As our bridleway is wide and firm this could have been a road in former days along the north-west bank of the Exe to connect with an existing lane to Brampford Speke.

View of Upton Pyne

Woodrow Barton

Follow the track through the meadows with the river over on your left. When the way turns left towards a weir keep straight on through a small wooden gate – following the footpath sign – to walk through a little wood. Go through another wooden gate and keep straight on along the hillside with a fence on your right. Over the fence the parkland rises and you have a wonderful view of the south front of Pynes, 'Barton Park' in the novel. Built around 1720, from designs by Inigo Jones, all is ordered symmetry and grace. It is not difficult to imagine Sir John and Lady Middleton living here 'in a style of equal hospitality and elegance'.

Keep straight on until you come to a gate. Go through the gate and over a stile, then follow the fenced path as it bears right and takes you round a farmyard and through more gates to join a track through the park. Our track meets the drive to Pynes. Keep straight on down the drive following the footpath sign to cross the cattle grid by the lodge and meet the lane to Upton Pyne village. Turn right and walk up the hill back to the village enjoying beautiful views of the Creedy valley on your left.

I believe that the 'narrow winding valley of Allenham which issued from that of Barton' is the valley of the Creedy. Here, about a mile and a half from the cottage, was the Dashwoods' favourite village which became even more intriguing when they discovered that near the church the 'ancient respectable looking mansion which, by reminding them a little of Norland, interested their imagination' was the home of Willoughby's close relative, a Mrs Smith. Although Newton St Cyres is more than two miles from Pynes the church and mansion there do resemble Marianne's description in the novel and the village is enchanting.

From Cowley Bridge follow the A377 towards Crediton for about two miles to Newton St Cyres. Just past the Crown and Sceptre turn left following the car park sign. Turn left again into the car park. First, you might like to explore the church which stands high above the road almost immediately opposite. There is a great deal of interest in the church of

St Julietta and her son St Cyr including a monument to the Northcote family dated 1632 in which the daughters kneel behind their mother in descending order and the sons behind their father. If you follow the lane opposite the church signposted to St Cyres' station and Thorverton you will see the mansion on the left. But if you would like a really splendid view of the village, church and mansion and to walk the quiet narrow lanes as Elinor and Marianne knew them, turn right in front of the Crown and Sceptre to cross the bridge between white and pink colour-washed cottages and climb the hill. After only a short climb you will be able to look across to the village dominated by its church and mansion. Marianne, standing in the drawing room of the great house looking the other way, would, as she says, 'have a view of the church and village, and, beyond them, of those fine old hills we have so often admired'.

It is clear from *Sense and Sensibility* that Jane Austen reflects her own delight in the hills through the characters of Elinor and Marianne. The theme of the novel and its setting may to a certain extent be allowed to take the place of the letters Cassandra burnt and tell us part of the story of those unrecorded days in the Devon countryside.

Map 8

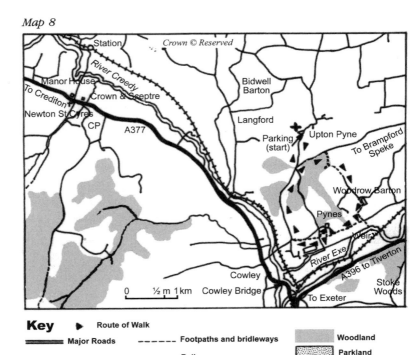

Key   ▶   **Route of Walk**

▬▬▬ **Major Roads**   – – – – **Footpaths and bridleways**   ▨ **Woodland**

▬▬▬ **Minor Roads**   ┼─┼─┼ **Railways**   ░░ **Parkland**

Park in small square in front of church in Upton Pyne. From square turn right to walk to junction with road to Brampford Speke. Turn left and follow lane for about a quarter of a mile to where woods end on right. Leave lane and turn right along bridleway, woods on right, field on left. Walk through Woodrow Barton farmyard, track bears right, straight on when track turns left to weir. Through gate, through wood, through another gate, straight on along hillside with fence on right. Past Pynes, through gate, follow path through more gates to track leading to the drive to Pynes. Straight on along drive to lodge to meet lane to Upton Pyne. Turn right to return to village.

Distance: about three miles. Very easy walking with views but be prepared for mud in wet weather.

9

Lyme Regis — 'Summers by the Sea'

'The prospect of spending future summers by the sea or in Wales is very delightful,' Jane wrote to Cassandra, in an attempt to reconcile herself to the thought of leaving Steventon to live in Bath. She loved the sea and visited the south coast many times. Her novels contain vivid touches that capture the sound of the sea, the light and movement of the waves and her own pleasure in exploring rocky coastlines and hidden bays. The ill-fated party from Uppercross in *Persuasion*, catching their first glimpse of the water, pause, 'lingering only, as all must linger and gaze on a first return to the sea'. Although in her last, unfinished novel *Sanditon*, Jane pokes fun at Mr Parker, so eager to abandon his snug, inland homestead to reside in his cliff-top village, 'our hill, our health-breathing hill', she allows her heroine, the sensible Charlotte, to find 'amusement enough in standing at her ample Venetian window, and looking over the miscellaneous foreground of unfinished buildings, waving linen, and tops of houses, to the sea, dancing and sparkling in sunshine and freshness'. As *Sanditon* depicts, the benefits of the seaside had been discovered afresh in Jane's time. But for her, a visit to the coast did not imply dressing elegantly to walk the fashionable promenade or indulging in drinking spa water and bathing in an attempt to cure real or imaginary diseases. She liked to sit on the beach, watching the ebb and flow of the tide, in 'unwearied contemplation' and take her usual long walks over the cliffs to neighbouring villages. She enjoyed sea bathing so much that once, at Lyme Regis, she stayed in so long that later in the day she found, to her surprise, she was 'unreasonably tired'. As she so seldom admits to any kind of fatigue she must have stayed in the water a long time indeed.

After Jane and Cassandra had accompanied their parents to Sidmouth in the summer of 1801 and spent part of the following summer on holiday in Dawlish and Teignmouth, Jane paid her first visit to Lyme Regis in the November of 1803.

The little seaside town delighted her. Evidently her parents and Cassandra shared the same feelings for the following September they paid another visit to Lyme, accompanied by her lively brother Henry and his wife Eliza. When, eleven years later, Jane sets part of her tender love story *Persuasion* in Lyme, her own happy memories of the glorious scenery surrounding the town overcome her scruples as a novelist. The party from Uppercross arrive for their first visit, like Jane herself, in November. Recalling her own impressions, for a moment she is carried away and forgets her characters. 'A very strange stranger it must be,' she writes, 'who does not see charms in the immediate environs of Lyme, to make him wish to know it better.' With delight she recalls, 'Charmouth . . . with its high grounds and extensive sweeps of country', 'the woody varieties of the cheerful village of Up Lyme' and 'Pinny, with its green chasms between romantic rocks . . . .' After a walk around Lyme it is easy to understand why Jane felt and wrote as she did. It is indeed fascinating. Apart from the old town itself, tucked in the steep-sided valley of the Lym, precariously balanced on its unstable blue lias and firmly buttressed against the force of the waves, a little to the west of the town a cluster of houses overlook its famous Cobb. This is not a harbour in the true sense of the word — there is no natural inlet — but a massive stone wall, shaped like a crooked elbow curving round Lyme to protect the fishing boats from the prevailing south-west winds. The north side is protected by another, detached wall which you approach from across the sands. A tiny square at the foot of

View of the Cobb, Lyme Regis

Cobb Hill stands at the approach to the Cobb, and close by, tradition states, Jane and her family took lodgings. So we will begin our walk at the Cobb, then follow in Jane's footsteps to Lyme to ramble in Charmouth fields and enjoy the lovely countryside she recalled so vividly.

You can park beside the Cobb itself, but it is better at busy times to use Holmbush car park a short distance away at the junction of Cobb Road and Pound Street. With the car park on your right, walk towards the top of Cobb Road. Just before the turning, follow the footpath sign right, to the Cobb. Now you have a splendid view of a toy-like harbour below, the humped sea wall, with its two broad causeways at different levels forming the upper and lower Cobb protecting the yachts and fishing boats at anchor. Descend the steep hill to the square. Ahead of you runs the Cobb wall as irresistible to walk along as Jane found it over a hundred and seventy years ago! On 14 September 1804 she writes to Cassandra (who had just left for Ibthorpe) that she had just paid a visit on a certain Miss Armstrong and that 'We afterwards walked together for an hour on the Cobb'. Miss Armstrong, who, Jane remarks, 'is considerably genteeler than her parents', may have provided her with a few ideas for the characters of the Miss Musgroves in *Persuasion*. She writes of the Musgrove family: 'The father and mother were in the old English style, and the young people in the new. Mr and Mrs Musgrove were a very good sort of people; friendly and hospitable, not much educated, and not at all elegant. Their children had more modern minds and manners.' If you look across the water to where the older part of the Cobb wall, distinguished by its

Granny's Teeth, the Cobb, Lyme Regis

dark, oval stones, curves towards the harbour entrance, you will see a very steep flight of solid stone steps jutting out of the inner wall. These are the famous 'Granny's Teeth' from which, in *Persuasion*, the headstrong Louisa insists on jumping into Captain Wentworth's arms. We can imagine Jane and Miss Armstrong carefully descending the steps, then our novelist recalling them to use as the centre piece of an incident which was to lead Captain Wentworth back to his devoted Anne, to feel 'that a persuadable temper might sometimes be as much in favour of happiness as a very resolute one'. For, as Louisa jumps the second time, crying, 'I am determined I will', Captain Wentworth misses her and 'she fell on the pavement on the Lower Cobb, and was taken up lifeless'. Results were not as disastrous as they appeared, but as you walk along the Cobb and perhaps descend the steps, you will agree that the foolhardy Louisa was fortunate to survive.

History records that a harbour of some kind has stood in this improbable position, fully exposed to the force of the Channel winds and tides since early in the fourteenth century. From these walls, the townspeople watched Drake skirmish with ships of the Armada in 1588, and the Duke of Monmouth make his ill-fated landing in 1685. Forty years earlier the Cobb had been bombarded by Royalist ships as Lyme withstood a six-week-long siege. From the end of the Cobb you have a perfect view of the colourful town at the foot of its wooded valley. Each side of the town reveals sharply contrasting scenery. To the east runs a long, undulating chain of slate blue lias, barred by golden sandstone, 'the very beautiful line of cliffs' which Jane comments upon. To the west, an open hillside reaches to the Cobb, then cliffs thickly wooded to the water's edge, where, writes Jane, 'a scene so wonderful and so lovely is exhibited'.

Return to the square, then turn right to walk round the small sandy bay towards Lyme. Follow the narrow street now called the Marine Parade, but in Jane's time known simply as the Walk. When the houses cease on the left you come to a delightful cliffside garden. You are now on the site of the lodging house, 'Wings', where Jane is said to have stayed. The garden was planted in her memory to celebrate the bicentenary of her birth and a play by Henry Chessel, *Miss Austen in Lyme*, was performed. Constance Hill describes the house as 'a long rambling white cottage' and quotes Miss Lefroy's description: 'There were two ground floors, one in its proper place and the other at the top of the house containing the bedrooms and back door, which latter opened on to the green hill behind.' There was a pretty sitting room, and if you climb the steps to one of the garden seats you will be able to enjoy the same view over the sea and the Cobb that Jane possibly saw. And on one of the garden walls facing the sea you will find a weathered stone bust of Jane. Jane was not too impressed by the lodgings, finding the offices inconvenient.

Opposite the garden – and Jane's window – is Bay Cottage, said to be the original of Captain Harville's snug little home in *Persuasion*. It is now a cafe but when I first walked this way, the cottage with its quaint corners and doors and windows strengthened with bars to withstand the Channel gales fitted Jane's description perfectly. 'In a small house, near the foot of an old pier of unknown date, were the Harvilles settled ... they all went indoors with their new friends and found rooms so small as none but those who invite from the heart could think capable of accommodating so many.' Perhaps Jane's neighbours invited her to join them.

Follow the walk round the bay – in Jane's time lined with bathing machines – past a group of pink-washed, thatched cottages to Cobb Gate at the foot of Broad Street, Lyme's 'principal street almost hurrying into the water.' Facing you, half surrounded by the sea, is the site of the Assembly Rooms, with arched recessed windows and crystal chandeliers, where Jane danced. Constance Hill records her impression of the rooms, commenting that they 'felt almost as if it were afloat, for nothing but blue sea and sky was to be seen from its many windows'. One evening, Mr Austen accompanied his wife and

The bust of Jane Austen, Lyme Regis

Jane to the rooms, but tiring early walked home 'with James and a lantern'. Jane and her mother stayed an hour longer, Jane dancing several times.

Turn right and walk along Bridge Street. You cross the Lym (known locally at this point as the Buddle) by a Norman bridge. Follow Church Street to the Charmouth Road. Lyme's steep, narrow streets are a fascinating mixture of colour-washed cottages, elegant eighteenth-century town houses with curved doorways and rounded bows and impressive mansions built of dove grey lias. Tunnels reached by steps beneath dark archways, lead to secluded gardens and hidden alleys, to old mills and crumbling flower-hung walls, reminders of the town's twelve hundred years of history. Follow the Charmouth road until you come to Spittles Lane on the right, opposite the cemetery. Just past the Lane, in the corner of the field you will see a small wooden stile. Go right, over the stile and follow the field path running diagonally ahead up the hillside through two gaps in hedges, the first with a stile and the second with a gate and a sign 'Charmouth Coast Path'. Follow this sign to a stile and footpath sign in front of an old wood at the top of the hill. As you climb high into Charmouth fields, a wonderful view of Lyme, the Cobb reaching into the sea behind, opens at your feet. We can imagine Jane enjoying walks and views like these as she explored the cliffs with her handsome, brilliant brother Henry, who, she remarks, 'could not help being amusing'. Henry enjoyed their walks too, so much so, Jane writes, that the next year he still 'talks of the rambles we took together last summer with pleasing affection'. I believe there is something of Henry in all Jane's witty male characters – not least in Henry Crawford. Henry has been accused of a tendency to moralise, particularly in his short memoir of Jane, but this would not be foreign to his generally attractive personality. In *Northanger Abbey*, Henry Tilney, so quick to advise the simple Catherine on the principles of the picturesque, combines these attributes. Henry has lent more than his name to several of his sister's portraits.

From the stile at the top of the hill the view over Lyme is even more spectacular and there is a well placed seat from which to enjoy it. To continue our walk turn left and follow the path along the edge of the trees. This is 'The Spittles', National Trust property, so you can wander at will along the many tempting paths that criss-cross beneath stands of tall pines, and groves of oaks, beech and sycamores. Our way lies through the gate ahead, down Timber Hill, and over the A3052 into Colway Lane. Follow this narrow, high-banked way as it plunges steeply down to the Lym to join the Roman Road at Horn Bridge. Turn left here to follow the streamside. The little river runs tree-shaded, bordered by twisting tree roots planted with ferns. On the opposite side, green meadows run down to the water. Cross Woodmead Road and follow the lane ahead, still by the stream. When the lane runs into the water, turn right over a bridge, and, with the stream now on your left, follow the path over a small green. The old mill opposite, now converted into flats, is interestingly named 'Jordan', a reminder that this name was given to this part of the river by early Baptists. The green was known as 'Paradise'. As we walk into the heart of Lyme we pass more old mills. In medieval days, Lyme was

View of Lyme Regis

famous for its cloth making, the waters of the Lym being harnessed for energy. Bear left to walk up Mill Green Road which curves right downhill. At the foot of the road keep ahead to follow a most attractive footpath signed 'Riverside Walk' which runs between the Lym and an artificial water-course which carries water to the top of the mill wheel. Across the Lym is a tiny garden reached by a small bridge, planted with apple trees and backed by a crumbling stone wall. In the centre of the garden a stone surround protects a well which was the water supply for a medieval hospital for lepers which stood on this site. Follow this path round past the restored Town Mill and walk up Coombe Street. Turn right to follow Bridge Street back to the foot of Broad Street.

Turn right and walk up Broad Street. Among the many charming houses, you see the two inns Jane mentions in *Persuasion*. They are the Three Cups on the left, with its rounded bows, and facing it, the Royal Lion with its angular windows projecting over the pavement. Between the inns, the party from Uppercross saw the servant dressed in mourning, in attendance on an interesting-looking stranger. Constance Hill believes that Jane had the Royal Lion in mind as their hotel. From their room, in the bay on the first floor, they could watch the stranger's curricle brought round to the front from the inn yard and 'all kindly watch him as far up the hill as they could'. There are recent theories that Jane may herself have lodged in a building on the other side of the road.

At the top of Broad Street, bear left along the A3052, Pound Street, for a short way, past the former Regent cinema. Now turn left through the gate into Langmoor Gardens and take this lovely way over the cliffside park, across the hill to join Cobb Road almost opposite the car park where we began our walk. We have walked only four miles, but our visit to Lyme has taken us out to sea along a medieval wall, round a fascinating old town, and high on to the cliffs. I think you will agree that it would be a 'strange stranger indeed' who did not enjoy so varied and so lovely a place as Lyme.

Map 9

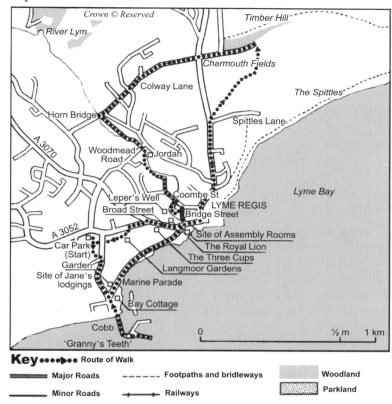

Key **•••▶••** Route of Walk

▬▬▬ Major Roads	– – – – Footpaths and bridleways	▨ Woodland
▬▬▬ Minor Roads	┼─┼─┼ Railways	▨ Parkland

*Park at junction of Cobb Road and Pound Street (Holmbush car park).
Walk towards the top of Cobb Road. Take footpath on right to Cobb. Explore
Cobb and return to Square. Turn right down Marine Parade (the Walk)
round Bay to Broad Street. Turn right along Bridge Street, then Church
Street and up the Charmouth Road. Just after Spittle Lane, go right over stile
in corner of field (Charmouth Fields). Climb field along diagonal path
through two gaps in hedges, second with sign 'Charmouth Coast Path'.
Follow this to a stile and footpath sign in front of wood. Turn left, down
Timber Hill, over A3052, down Colway Lane to Horn Bridge. Turn left by
river Lym. Cross Woodmead Road, follow lane ahead, turn right over
bridge and follow path down Mill Green Road, over road, to path between
the Lym and Mill leat. Pass Town Mill, walk up Coombe Street, right into
Bridge Street, right up Broad Street. At top, left along A3052 for a few yards
before turning left into Langmoor Gardens. Bear right through gardens to
Cobb Road and car park. Distance: about four miles.*

10

Southampton – Jane and the Navy

If Jane Austen had been a boy I believe it is quite possible that three members of the Austen family rather than two would have attended Portsmouth Naval Academy. In choosing the professions to be followed by her characters, Jane is careful to restrict herself to those she knows well, mainly those adopted by her own family. Clergymen on the whole fare badly – we recall the obsequious Mr Collins in *Pride and Prejudice* and the unpleasant oily Mr Elton in *Emma* – but her treatment of sailors is a different story. From her pages step the most charming naval characters from the young and dashing William Price in *Mansfield Park* to the genial, hearty Admiral Croft in *Persuasion*. Jane is even happy to allow her sailors their traditional roving eye. The irresistible Captain Wentworth is allowed to win back his sweet Anne at the close of *Persuasion*. In his *Memoir* her nephew comments 'with ships and sailors she felt herself at home, or at least could always trust to a brotherly critic to keep her right. I believe that no flaw has ever been found in her seamanship either in *Mansfield Park* or in *Persuasion*'. Moreover, Jane endows her sailors, and their wives, with special qualities. In *Persuasion*, the Crofts and the Harvilles impress Anne with their marital devotion and comradeship and the 'repose and domestic happiness' in their homes. Although Jane's stay in Southampton lasted only two-and-a-half years she lived close to the heart of this great port and met many naval people. They must have pleased her and confirmed the good opinion she received from her sailor brothers Frank and Charles.

After the death of her father in January 1805, there seemed no real reason why Jane, Cassandra and Mrs Austen should remain in Bath. In April Mrs Lloyd died and Martha came to live with them as a permanent member of their household. Possibly they lingered in Bath at the wish of the Leigh-Perrots but the following year came the possibility of an interesting move to Southampton. Frank, captain of the *Canopus*, had the misfortune (he wrote) to miss the Trafalgar action, but after a victory over the French at St Domingo had come home to marry Mary Gibson. The Austen ladies had not met Mary and it was decided that they should move into lodgings with Frank and Mary in Southampton. In July 1806 with what Jane recalls 'happy feelings of escape' they left Bath and after visits to various relatives, were in Southampton by the end of the year. They were delighted with Mary. But they were a large household — apart from the two families there was their cook Jenny, maid Molly, and Phoebe whose duties appear unspecified — and Mrs Austen's income, from her sons, was not great. Lodgings were expensive and they began to look for a house to rent. Early in 1807 they moved into what the *Memoir* calls 'a commodious old-fashioned residence' in Castle Square, inside the north-west corner of the old city walls. From here, narrow, medieval streets ran down to the town quay, bustling with preparations for war. Southampton Water and the river Itchen were thronged with merchant vessels and men o' war taking advantage of the double tides. But Southampton had more to offer than its historic streets, its ships and trade. In the middle of the eighteenth century, with the discovery of the benefits of drinking spa waters and sea bathing, 'the reign of salt water', as Jonas Hanway puts it, began. Southampton gained new life as a fashionable watering place. The patronage of George II's eldest son, Frederick, brought new prosperity. The towns-people began to fit up their homes for visitors 'in the neatest and genteelest manner' to quote an old guide book. The rich built a ring of large villas in the pleasant, wooded countryside around the town. Various attempts were made to convert the old seaport itself into a more 'polite' place: the streets were paved and lit, the houses numbered and traps for the unwary pedestrian, like open cellars and discharging spouts, were removed. The Austens found no difficulty in travelling to Southampton as good coach services operated from all important towns. Excellent inns (still to be seen) were built to accommodate travellers. Although Southampton could hardly rival Bath in magnificent architecture, it could offer Jane the advantages of circulating libraries, a theatre, frequent balls and concerts and fine shops. Jane enjoyed these and took special delight in long walks through the lovely countryside surrounding the town, beside Southampton Water and along the banks of the Itchen. Crossing the Itchen by ferry was a treat, and we hear of plans to visit Netley, Beaulieu and the Isle of Wight. Writing to Cassandra, then staying at Godmersham, she hopes Mrs Knight will not grow too fond of her sister because then 'we must remove to Canterbury which I should not like so well as Southampton'.

Jane already knew the town. At the age of seven she attended school here with Cassandra and their cousin Jane Cooper. After a few weeks she nearly died with a fever. In the December of 1793 she visited the town and in *Love and Friendship* a character refers to 'the dissipation of London, the luxuries of Bath, and the stinking fish of Southampton'. Stinking or not, we find Jane sending presents of 'soals' to her friends.

So soon after her father's death and with no settled home, it is not surprising that Jane did not continue her novel writing at Castle Square. She left *The Watsons* unfinished and perhaps she was discouraged by the fact that *Susan* (published by Henry after her death as *Northanger Abbey*) which had been sold to the Bath publishers, Crosby and Sons, in the spring of 1803, had still not appeared. Her early letters from Southampton, written while in lodgings, betray a certain sadness. Some of her remarks have an almost bitter note which suggest she was unhappy. With Frank, she calls on the Lances who lived in a large house 'among the woods on the other side of the Itchen'. She comments on Mrs Lance: 'They live in a handsome style and are rich, and she seemed to like being rich, and we gave her to understand that we were far from being so; she will soon feel therefore that we are not worth her acquaintance.' Even brother James, in spite of being such 'an excellent man', annoyed her 'in walking about the house and banging the doors'. The weather, of course, is bad. 'I expect a severe March, a wet April and a sharp May,' she predicts. But her happy nature reasserts itself as she describes to Cassandra how they are all preparing for the move to Castle Square. Frank, in his handy sailor fashion, is busy making beds and knotting fringes. We recall the industrious Captain Harville: 'He drew, he varnished, he

Bargate, Southampton

carpentered, he glued; he made tops for the children, he fashioned new netting needles and pins with improvements.' The day draws closer and a certain Mrs Day is called to make the final preparations. This short walk, about two miles round the most fascinating part of medieval Southampton, follows Jane and her family to the site of their new house.

We begin from the Bargate in the High Street. This was built by the Normans in the twelfth century as the northern entrance to the town. After the disastrous French raid in 1338 it was strengthened, and the existing walls to the north and east of the town continued around its seaward southern and western sides. Long stretches of these magnificent walls remain and we follow them round the old town. Facing the north front of the Bargate, turn right into Bargate Street. With the city walls on your left, cross the road, Castle Way. Now you are looking at the tower which fortified the north-west corner of the Walls. It still stands high on grass-covered embankments and away to the south runs the whole length of the western defences. In Jane's time the sea lapped a narrow foreshore beneath these towers, broken only by two small quays projecting from the Watergate and Westgate. Bear left through the small arch ahead, then right towards the tower. Turn left and walk along the top of the walls. You will see the Masonic Hall ahead and to the right of it runs a terrace of eighteenth-century cottages, called 'Forest View' – a reminder that where we now see docks, cranes and warehouses, Jane looked out over the waters of West Bay to the trees of the New Forest crowding thickly to the shore. Turn left in front of the hall and cross a parking area towards an archway in a long, curving stone wall. Go through the archway and you are standing close to a small triangular space at the junction of several roads which is Castle Square. The wall, curving away on the left, is part of the defensive bailey wall of a fourteenth-century royal castle which once stood close by. This was demolished but in 1804 the Marquis of Lansdowne built a large castellated mansion in Gothic style which filled a considerable part of the square. Jane's nephew records that her house overlooked 'the little space that remained of the open square'. 'The Marchioness had a light phaeton drawn by six, and sometimes by eight little ponies,' he recalls. 'It was a delight to me to look down from the window and see this fairy equipage put together.' Constance Hill thought the northern side of the square the most likely site of the house, but R A Austen-Leigh believes it stood either in front of the former Juniper Berry Inn, since renamed (Upper Bugle Street did not exist then) or a little to the south of the inn beside a lane which connected the square with Simnel Street close to the western shore. What is certain is that their house had a beautiful garden, running back to the city wall with steps giving them access to the promenade along the top. 'Our garden is the best in town!' writes Jane enthusiastically. There was a gravel walk bordered by roses and she meant to plant better kinds and, because her favourite poet Cowper had described it, a syringa. Wine-making was evidently still important. 'The border under the terrace wall is clearing away to receive currants and gooseberry bushes and a spot is found very proper for raspberries.' In the square, their company rapidly increased to include Admiral Bertie, his wife and daughter and other naval families who knew Frank. On the evening of 4 October they were threatened by a fire which broke out in Webbes, the pastry cooks in the High Street, but fortunately the flames did not reach them. But at the end of that month, real tragedy came to the Austen household with the death of Edward's wife, Elizabeth. Cassandra was at Godmersham with the bereaved family and Jane, writing with great love and sympathy, asks that Edward and George, her nephews at school in Winchester might be sent to her. They arrived and Jane did all in her power to make them happy. 'Spillikins, paper ships, riddles, conundrums and cards, with watching the flow and ebb of the river, and now and then a stroll out, keep us well employed.' One day she took her nephews for a 'little water party' on the Itchen. We will follow them part of the way.

Walk past the inn down Upper Bugle Street into the square in front of the lovely church of St Michael. Like

Jane, you pass Tudor House, a magnificent early sixteenth-century building on your right. Continue down lower Bugle Street between eighteenth-century houses with rounded windows and Dutch gables. Cross the top of Westgate Street. You might like to make a short detour down to the Westgate with the Tudor Merchant's Hall standing beside it. This gate led to the quay where part of Henry V's army embarked for Agincourt and the Pilgrim Fathers sailed in the *Speedwell* and the *Mayflower*. Close by, Jane would see the Long Rooms where summer balls were held.

The inn close to the old city wall, possibly on or near the site of the Austens' house, Castle Square

On the right you pass the Pilgrim Fathers memorial and on the left, facing the town quay you pass the fourteenth-century wool house. Jane might have heard foreign accents from inside the wool house as in her time it was used as a prison for French prisoners of war. She would turn left here to follow a long causeway called 'The Beach' running west and planted with trees. At the eastern end of this fashionable promenade she came to Crosshouse, a round building to shelter travellers using the Itchen ferry. She embarked with her nephews and they rowed up the Itchen to look over a man o' war — a 74 — at Northam bridge. There can be no doubt that Aunt Jane enjoyed the trip as much as her nephews. Leave the Wool House on your left and cross the bottom of French Street. Here Jane visited the theatre. Opposite French Street was the town quay. From here, hoys to Portsmouth sailed three times a week. These would be useful for Frank and it is pleasant to imagine Jane going with him and acquiring the knowledge of Portsmouth dock yard she reveals in *Mansfield Park*. We can imagine her watching 'the effects of the shadows pursuing each other . . . the ships at Spithead and the island beyond, with the ever-varying hues of the sea now at high water, dancing in its glee and dashing against the ramparts'.

Bear a little left down another narrow, medieval street, Porter's Lane, past the ruins of a Norman merchant's house. Continue down Winkle Lane to Gods House Gate, built in the thirteenth century. Gods House, the massive stone building adjoining, was built in 1185 by the port reeve, Gervase le Riche, as a shelter for poor travellers and the aged, sick and poor. Return through the arch and walk immediately right. The most ancient part of Southampton's walls runs beside you on the right. Go down the steps into Briton Street, turn left and walk back to the High Street. Turn right towards the Bargate. On the right you pass the old coaching inn, the Red Lion, then the ruins of the fourteenth-century Holyrood Church, always known as 'the sailor's church' and after its destruction in 1940, preserved as a memorial to those who

Print: Northam Bridge and a man-of-war

The Dolphin Hotel

served in the Merchant Navy. Now you will see, projecting over the pavement the large, rounded bows of the Dolphin hotel. The first floor bow is part of the Long Room where Jane attended balls during the winter season. On 9 December 1808 she writes to Cassandra: 'Our ball was rather more amusing than I expected . . . you will not expect to hear that *I* was asked to dance — but I was!' Of another ball the following January she writes: 'We were very well entertained . . . the Miss Lances have partners, Capt. D'auvernes friend appeared in regimentals, Caroline Maitland had an officer to flirt with and Mr John Harrison was deputed by Capt. Smith . . . to ask me to dance.' Opposite the corner of East Street is the site of All Saints, Jane's parish church. Built in classical style in 1795 it was destroyed in 1940. Jane and her family were regular attenders. With impish delight, Jane imagines an affair between Cassandra and the rector, Dr Mant. Possibly this was because he *was* such a worthy man, a former head-master of King Edward's Grammar School, an excellent preacher with a wife of his own and ten children! We are now back at the Bargate. Jane's walks ranged north to Bellevue and the Polygon, where an expensive project to build homes for the wealthy had been left unfinished, and east over the Itchen to Chessel.

Early in 1809, Edward offered his mother the choice of a home, either on his Godmersham Estates or at Chawton in Hampshire. Mrs Austen chose Chawton. For Jane, this would mean a return to the peaceful, slower-paced country life she loved and her letters sparkle with joyful anticipation. Perhaps she began to think she might write again as in the last week of her stay in Southampton, 5 April 1809, she wrote to Crosby and Sons enquiring about the publication of *Susan*. She could have the manuscript back, they replied, for the price they paid for it, £10. Jane may have been disappointed as she did not reply. But her great writing years were now very close. The Austens left Southampton in April, and, after visits to Bookham and Godmersham as planned, they moved into their Chawton home in July 1809.

Map 10

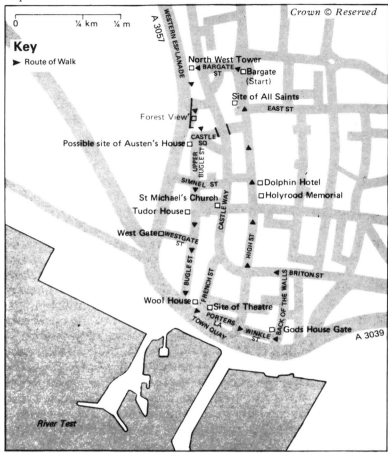

Start from the Bargate in the High Street. Facing the north front, turn right into Bargate Street. Cross Castle Way. Turn left and walk along city walls. Turn left in front of the Masonic Hall and cross a parking area to go through an archway into Castle Square. Walk past the inn down Upper Bugle Street, past St Michael's church on left and Tudor House on right. Cross the top of Westgate Street (short detour to Westgate). Continue down Lower Bugle Street to town quay. Turn left, past the Wool House, over the bottom of French Street. Bear left down Porter's Lane and Winkle Lane, through archway by Gods House. Turn right with city walls on right and walk down back of the walls to Briton Street. Turn left to High Street. Turn right and walk up High Street back to the Bargate.
Distance: about two miles.

11

'Our Chawton Home'

'Everybody is acquainted with Chawton and speaks of it as a remarkably pretty village,' Jane wrote to Cassandra, anticipating their new life in Chawton Cottage. Jane was thirty-three when she moved in with her mother, Cassandra, and Martha Lloyd in July 1809. The cottage, homely and comfortable in its pretty garden, answered all their expectations. Jane was so delighted with her new home that she was inspired to write one of her rare pieces of verse about it. After congratulating Frank on the birth of his son, she continues:

> Our Chawton home, how much we find
> Already in it, to our mind;
> And how convinced that when complete
> It will all other houses beat
> That ever have been made or mended,
> With rooms concise, or rooms distended . . .

The cottage had six bedrooms, enough to house the people she loved on visits. Henry came, sometimes accompanied by friends from London, her sailor brothers, Edward with some of his children, although later he stayed in Chawton House, the Elizabethan manor close by which he owned. James was only seventeen miles away at Steventon and his daughter Anna recalls how often she drove through the leafy country lanes to the cottage. Acquaintance with friends from Steventon, including the Terrys and the Digweeds, was renewed and their new circle of acquaintances in Chawton included the same kind of country folk: the Middletons who rented Chawton Manor, and the Benns, the large family of the vicar of nearby Farringdon. At home there was much to do; a share of the household chores, sewing both for the family and 'Edward's poor', and an increasing number of young nephews and nieces to care for and entertain. Once again Jane could enjoy the settled, happy, useful life she loved, surrounded by the pleasant Hampshire countryside that was home to her. In such an atmosphere her mind could return to its story-telling. These Chawton years saw the revision of her earlier novels, *Sense and Sensibility* and *Pride and Prejudice*, and witnessed the great novels of her maturity: *Mansfield Park*, *Emma* and *Persuasion*.

Chawton Cottage

Today, Chawton is still a most attractive village. Jane's home, Chawton Cottage, beautifully restored, can be visited. Chawton is about a mile south of Alton. Formerly the main road from Winchester to London and the Gosport road met in the village. Jane's home stood beside the junction of the two roads, overlooking a pond. Now, although the pond is no longer there, it is easy to recapture the serenity of earlier years as the main road bypasses the village. Follow the signs for Chawton and park. Buses stop at either end of the village on the A32 Bypass. Jane's home is quite a substantial house though simply built of brick with double rows of plain sash windows. Two dormers break the line of the deep-tiled roof. Edward had some alterations made which Caroline, James Austen's second daughter, describes: 'A good sized entrance and two sitting rooms made the length of the house, all intended originally to look upon the road; but a large drawing room window was blocked up and turned into a bookcase, and another opened at the side which gave view to only turf and trees and a high wooden fence and hornbeam hedge shut out the Winchester Road, which skirted the whole length of the little domain.'

You enter the garden from the road through a wrought-iron gate, then pass Edward's new window to go into the house by the side door. From a small entrance, you walk into the Austens' drawing room. The room is low with a central beam and an attractive four-arched window overlooking the garden. The whole atmosphere recalls Jane and her family. In a case you will find the two topaz crosses Charles brought for his sisters with prize money, a gift Jane remembers when, in *Mansfield Park*, William Price buys a cross for his sister, Fanny. Beside the crosses is a bracelet that belonged to Jane, delicately made of tiny blue beads with a gold filigree clasp. The piano, with one of Jane's music books on it, is similar to the one she promises Cassandra they will have at the cottage. 'Yes, yes, we will have a pianoforte,' she writes, 'as good a one as can be got for thirty guineas, and will practice country dances that we may have some amusement for our nephews

Chawton Cottage. Top: the drawing room

*Above: The dining parlour showing the small rectangular
table where Jane is believed to have written her novels*

*Right: Jane's bedroom. Part of the plaster has been removed to
show the timber construction of the cottage*

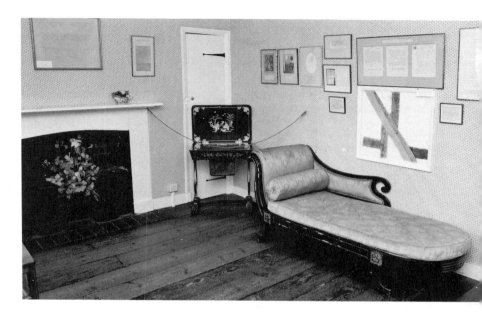

and nieces, when we have the pleasure of their company.' She set part of each day aside for regular practice.

You cross a vestibule containing reference books on Jane Austen and also one of her manuscript music books to the Austens' dining parlour. Here, in a room with a door opening directly on to the street, Jane wrote her novels. It is said that the other door, leading to the back of the house, creaked, and she asked that it should not be oiled. The noise warned her that someone was coming so that she could quickly slip her small sheets of paper out of sight and so keep her authorship a secret. The cupboard on the left of the fireplace was probably used to keep their tea, coffee and sugar. Perhaps Jane had the key, for, Caroline recalls: 'At 9 o'clock she made breakfast – that was her part of the household work. The tea and sugar stores were under her charge – and the wine – Aunt Cassandra did all the rest.' We can imagine Jane filling a little copper kettle like the one standing in the fireplace today and setting it to boil. While they ate, there was little privacy. A friend wrote to Fanny: 'I heard of the Chawton party looking very comfortable at breakfast, from a gentleman who was travelling by their door in a post-chaise.'

Jane's bedroom is at the top of the stairs on the left. It is a small, comfortable-looking room, crossed by a beam, with a square, small-paned window looking over the garden. Two large cupboards, one used for washing purposes and the other for clothes, stand each side of the original fireplace. A striking feature is a beautiful patchwork quilt Jane made with her mother. Both the design and the neatness of her sewing reveal the devotion to detail so characteristic of her writing. Across the corridor, Mrs Austen's room has two large windows looking across the village street towards the old Grey Friar Inn. No doubt, like Emma, Mrs Austen saw much to interest her in all the activities of village life. Another bedroom contains mementoes of Jane's sailor brothers. More rooms are devoted to a display of Jane's early manuscripts and pictures of her various homes. At the end of the corridor is a small costume museum, the models wearing clothes contemporary with her time. Cross the yard at the side of the house, past the well, to the bakehouse with its deep bread oven and old copper-lined wash tub. Here you will also see Jane's donkey cart.

Allow time to wander round the garden, restored to how it was in Jane's time and filled with many of the flowers, shrubs and trees she mentions. She writes to Cassandra in May, 1811: 'Our young piony at the foot of the fir tree has just blown and looks very handsome, and the whole of the shrubbery border will soon be gay with pinks and sweet williams.' Jane had a sharp eye for fruit too: 'I hear today that an apricot has been detected on one of the trees.' Could it have been a Moor Park like Mrs Norris planted? But evidently Jane's eye was not as sharp as Cassandra's. 'Yesterday,' Jane writes, 'I had the agreeable surprise of finding several scarlet strawberries quite ripe; had *you* been home this would have been a pleasure lost!' We can follow her steps round the garden beside the beech hedge, along the pleasant shrubbery walk that Isabel Lefroy, Anna's daughter, tells us was furnished 'with a rough bench or two where no

A corner of the bakehouse showing the bread oven and wash boiler

Jane's donkey cart

doubt Mrs Austen and Cassandra and Jane spent many a summer afternoon'. No doubt they did; there are many garden scenes in Jane's novels. Gardens, particularly shrubberies, were ideal places to read letters, calm agitated feelings or just enjoy a little privacy in those days of large households. In such a garden Mr Knightley declared his love to Emma.

Jane spent many hours at Chawton House, particularly when Edward visited with his family. Our walk follows her there. From the cottage gate turn right and take the old road which runs between the grounds of Chawton House and a row of ancient 'cruck' cottages. The parkland rises gently on your left, dotted with tall branching chestnuts. Soon you come to a drive leading left over the meadows to Chawton House, always called the 'Great House' by the Austens. This is a fine Elizabethan mansion with a square Tudor porch and heavy mullioned windows. In Jane's time the hall was the large wainscoted room on the first floor with its great open fire place. It has the date of the Armada, 1588 engraved on the fireback. The room most closely associated with Jane is the oak room on the first floor which has a large window over the porch. We can imagine her here, talking to Fanny or playing with the younger children; perhaps telling them stories full of people, who, the children remembered, 'all had characters of their own'. Looking out of the window, she saw the wide grounds, and the approach to the house, an avenue of tall trees. She may have had Chawton House in mind when, in *Emma*, she describes Mr Knightley's home, Donwell. 'She viewed the respectable size and style of the building, its suitable, becoming, characteristic situation, low and sheltered; its ample gardens ... its abundance of timber in rows and avenues.' Jane records with pleasure how Edward is making a new garden behind the house.

To the right of the drive is the small grey stone church of St Nicholas. In the churchyard, on the south-east corner, you will find the graves of Cassandra and Mrs Austen. Inside, only the chancel and sanctuary survive from Jane's time.

When Jane arrived, the vicar was a bachelor, Mr Papillon. Just right for Jane said Mrs Knight. Much amused, Jane wrote to Cassandra, 'she may depend upon it, that I *will* marry Mr Papillon, whatever may be his reluctance or my own!' You will see the rectory facing the drive to Chawton House.

Our walk continues in Jane's footsteps to visit more clerical neighbours, the Benns at Farringdon. Surrounded as she was by clergy, this may have influenced her decision after the publication of *Sense and Sensibility* in 1811, and *Pride and Prejudice* in 1813, to write a novel to include her views on the church. She wrote to Cassandra: 'Now I will try to write of something else, and it shall be a complete change of subject – ordination – I am glad to find your enquiries have ended so well.' The novel was to be *Mansfield Park* and it is indeed different from her earlier work. Perhaps Jane felt that after the 'Light, and bright and sparkling' nature of *Pride and Prejudice* she should write more seriously, and concern herself with a heroine as different as possible from the brilliant and confident Elizabeth Bennet. Perhaps she felt it was time she gave the world an attractive clergyman. Although ordination and its duties is only one of several important themes running through *Mansfield Park* it is central to the story. The eighteenth-century church has no sharper critic than Jane, so aware of the dangers that beset both the clergyman and his congregation if he abuses his duties. She must be voicing many a family discussion as well as her own views when her Edmund defines his ideal clergyman to the worldly Crawfords, supported by his father, Sir Thomas, who insists that a good clergyman must live among his parishioners 'and prove himself by constant attention their well-wisher and friend'.

From Chawton House drive, turn left and follow the old road past a barrier. At the end of the road keep ahead along a narrow footpath through the trees and cross a stile on the left. Bear right along the grassy path and cross a final stile to the open hillside. Bear diagonally a little left up the field towards a wood.

Chawton House

Cross a stile by a gate into the wood to follow a path through a narrow belt of oak trees. Now, running straight ahead, you will see a raised path. With the hedge on your right, follow the path as it climbs to a pine wood. A rutted path through the wood leads you to an avenue of yew trees. Follow the yews downhill towards Farringdon village, sheltered in a fold of the downs ahead. Cross a lane. Now you will see a low brick wall on the left. Immediately before the wall, a signposted path turns left for Farringdon church. Bear left then right to walk through the churchyard with its magnificent hollow yews, to this fascinating Norman church. The lowest part of the tower, with its deep-set lancet windows, dates back to the early thirteenth century. Two rectors (one was John Benn) held the living from 1797 to 1919!

Leave the church by the south porch and walk down to the lane ahead. When you reach the lane turn left past some picturesque black and white half-timbered cottages. Take the first lane on the right, Crows Lane, and at the end, opposite the Rose and Crown, turn right again. A few yards further, opposite a house called Brownings Orchard, you will see path on the left. Turn left along this sunken lane which bears right past a stile then left to bring you into the open, high on a hillside. Turn right and follow the bridleway downhill then right to the A32. Turn left and follow the road for about a quarter of a mile until you come to a lane on the right signposted 'Farringdon and Kitcombe Kennels'. Follow this quiet lane as it runs along the side of a shallow valley with lush meadows sloping up to hanging oak and beech woods. This remote and lovely place can have changed little since Jane's time. When the way divides, bear a little left along a small lane with the wood on your right. When you reach a junction of several paths, keep to the lane (now a track and unsigned) as it bears left through hazel thickets then turns right to bring you to a minor road. Turn right and follow the road downhill until you come to a turning to Pies Farm first on the left. Do not follow the lane to the farm, but take the unsigned path to the left of it. This brings you to a beautiful oak wood.

Immediately on entering the wood turn right along a track running along the edge of the wood. This enchanting path leads you under the spreading boughs of oak and beech trees through glades of bracken and heather and groves of graceful silver birches. The path runs through the wood for a little over a mile, before it leaves the trees to become a narrow lane which runs downhill past Woodside Farm. Jane knew these ways well. The farms provided food for special occasions. In May 1811 Jane wrote to Cassandra: 'We shall have peas soon – I mean to have them with a couple of ducks from Wood Barn and Maria Middleton towards the end of next week.' Wood Barn is close by. The lane bears right, then left to meet the A32. Cross the main road and follow the gravel track immediately ahead towards Farringdon church. Before you come to the church, in front of a large barn, look for the path we originally came down into Farringdon, leading uphill on the left. Turn left and retrace our route through the wood and over the field to the A32. When you come to the main road, turn right and make certain you go down the steps to the old road so that you can enjoy this peaceful way back past Chawton House to the village.

Jane Austen's house is a private museum administered by the Jane Austen Memorial Trust. The house was donated to the Trust as a memorial to Lieutenant Philip John Carpenter who was killed in action in 1944. There is a large public car park opposite the house behind the Grey Friar car park.

The house is open to visitors 1st March to 31st December. January and February it is open Saturdays and Sundays. Closed Christmas Day and Boxing Day. Times: 11 a.m. until 4.30 p.m. There is a fee for admission. Do visit the excellent bookshop.

Very good morning coffee, lunches and teas at Cassandra's Cup opposite the house.

Key ••••▶•• Route of Walk

════════ Major Roads   ‒ ‒ ‒ ‒ ‒ ‒ Footpaths and bridleways   [ ] Woodland

──────── Minor Roads   +——+ Railways   [ ] Parkland

Map 11

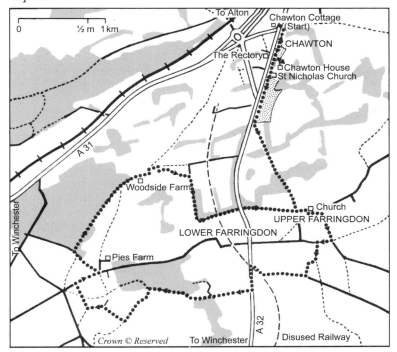

Park in Chawton car park opposite Jane Austen's house beyond the parking
for the Grey Friar pub. Visit the cottage then turn right along the old road
beside Chawton Manor grounds. At end continue along narrow footpath,
cross stile on left and bear right to cross a final stile to the open hillside.
Bear a little left up the field to stile leading to path through narrow wood.
Follow raised path straight ahead which climbs to a pine wood. Keep
straight on through avenue of yews to cross a lane. Just before brick wall
follow very narrow path left through churchyard to Farringdon church.
Leave by south porch, to road, turn left, then first right, then right again
opposite Rose and Crown. A few yards down road, turn up a footpath on
left. Follow this to open hillside, turn right and walk down to A32. Turn left
for a short way, cross road and take lane on right signposted 'Farringdon
and Kitcombe Kennels'. When this divides, take lane on left, wood on right.
This leads to minor road. Turn right then left beside turning to Pies Farm.
Lane leads to wood. Turn right along edge of wood to lane down past
Woodside Farm. Lane bears right, then left to A32. Cross road, follow track
opposite towards Farringdon. In front of a large barn, turn left up our
original track into Farringdon. Retrace route back to Chawton village.
Distance: about seven miles. Easy walking.

12

Walking to Alton, Wyards Farm and Chawton Park

'Young ladies are delicate plants,' says the kindly valetudinarian Mr Woodhouse in *Emma*, horrified to discover that Jane Fairfax has been walking in the rain. His creator did not share his views. Jane Austen's heroines, with the possible exception of Fanny Price, enjoy excellent health and have no objection to plenty of fresh air and exercise. We have only to think of Elizabeth Bennet running three miles over muddy fields to visit her sister and Emma 'the picture of grown-up health'. Even the delicate Fanny, whose bodily weakness presents a strong contrast with her firm moral sense, knows that fresh air will be good for her. They reflect the opinion of Jane herself.

Most days, Isabel Lefroy tells us, Jane and Cassandra could be seen walking in the countryside around Chawton. When, weakened by ill-health, Jane could no longer walk she drove her donkey cart and even attempted a ride on the donkey. In her letters she frequently mentions walking to Alton to shop and post letters, to Wyards Farm to visit Anna, who married and settled there in 1815, and to Chawton Park wood, then known for its magnificent beech trees. Today, we can still follow in her footsteps. Very quickly we leave the busy world of motorways behind to enjoy the peace of the quiet valleys shaded by deep woods where Jane rambled with her sister. As she trod these retired ways we can imagine her

Right: Chawton Park Wood

finding in their beauty the refreshment she needed to plan her stories and create her characters.

Park in Chawton again. The first part of our walk follows Jane to Alton. With Chawton Cottage on your left, walk through the attractive village, past the old forge now a craft shop. On your right you pass the village hall with its memorial to those who served in both world wars. Some of the names are familiar from Jane's letters. Many of the cottages we pass, half-timbered beneath deep thatch, or built with simple eighteenth-century elegance with fine doorways and rounded windows, Jane will have known. No doubt, like us, she enjoyed their colourful gardens and the folk she met. She reflects her pleasure in village life in *Emma* set in and around the pleasant village of Highbury. While she was writing this novel in 1814, Anna sent her part of her novel to criticise. Jane wrote back: 'You are now collecting your people delightfully, getting them exactly into such a spot as is the delight of my life; 3 or 4 families in a country village is the very thing to work on.' Jane's interest in village life was not purely literary. She tells Cassandra an amusing story. While out in her donkey cart she met a neighbouring farmer, Mr Woolls. Jane writes: 'I talked of it being bad weather for the hay — he returned me the comfort of its being much worse for the wheat!'

At the end of the lane keep straight on. Go down the steps and through the subway to rejoin the old road to Alton. When our way is crossed by the B3006, keep straight on, under the railway, following the signs for the town centre. On the left you pass a wide green fringed by chestnut trees called the Butts, a reminder of the days when practice with the longbow was a compulsory part of the upbringing of every boy. Walk up Alton High Street with its wealth of old inns proving its importance as a market and former coaching centre. Above many modern shop fronts, the eighteenth-century façades remain as Jane knew them. On one of her shopping expeditions, Jane experienced the same feelings she attributes to Emma who, having accompanied her rather silly young friend Harriet to Fords to buy material for a new gown, has to help her make a sensible choice and tell Mrs Ford where to send the parcel. 'I had just left off writing and put on my things for walking to Alton,' she tells Cassandra, 'when Anna and her friend Harriot (Benn) called in their way thither, so we went together. Their business was to provide mourning, against the King's death ... I am not sorry to be back again, for the young ladies had a great deal to do – and without much method in doing it.'

Turn left up Market Street opposite The Swan hotel which leads to the old square surrounded by inns. Turn right down Amery Street. On the left you will see a long, low house with an eighteenth-century faade concealing what is obviously a much older building. Follow Amery Street to Alton's splendid nine-hundred-year-old church which stands high, a little to the right of the road. Turn right and cross the churchyard to enter the building by the south porch. Although most of this fascinating church was built in the fifteenth century, it incorporates part of earlier churches built on the site including the tower and nave of a Norman building. The pillars of the Norman tower are delightfully decorated with carvings of birds and animals, among them a wolf gnawing a bone, a dove and two donkeys with their heels in the air. They would certainly have amused Jane and she would know too about the famous battle in Alton church. In 1643, the Cavaliers in Alton were surprised by a party of Roundheads. After fighting their way through the town, the Roundheads finally drove the Cavaliers under Colonel Boles to take refuge in the church. They shot their way in and killed the Colonel as he made his last stand by the pulpit. The battle has been re-enacted recently. Like us, Jane must have seen the church door, heavily pock-marked with bullet holes, and the remains of lead bullets embedded in the columns of the Norman tower.

Leave the church by the south porch and retrace your steps over the churchyard to Amery Street. Across the road, to the left of the Amery Farm Veterinary Group building runs a footpath. Cross the road and follow the path which brings you

The carved capitals in Alton Church

to an open hillside with a lake, overgrown with willows and rushes, in the valley on your left. Turn left to bring you close to the water. Among the islands, the channels are covered in a profusion of wild mint and cress. These are the fresh-water springs that feed the little River Wey which flows through Alton. With its network of tiny paths this is a children's paradise. The path bears right to follow the streamside to a crosspath. Turn left and follow the same path as it curves left to the Basingstoke road. Turn left and walk for only a few yards before turning right into Ackender Road. Take the first right again into Queen's Road. Straight ahead you will now see a footpath. Follow this to cross a lane then to the B3006. Immediately over the road you will see a gravel track. Cross the road to the gravel, ignore the bridleway sign for Beech and take the narrow footpath on the right which bears round the edge of Ackender Wood, to wander along the side of a shallow valley. Look over the fields on your right and you will see a deep-roofed farmhouse nestling among the trees in the valley. This is Wyards Farm, once Anna's home.

Anna had special claims on her Aunt Jane's affection. Her mother had died when she was two, upsetting the child so much that she had to be taken to Steventon rectory to be comforted. She grew up very attractive, but wilful and headstrong. In her letters Jane refers to her as 'an Anna with variations'. She loved company but enjoyed what Jane called 'plenty of the miscellaneous unsettled sort of happiness which seems to suit her best'. Witty and intelligent, she borrowed romances from the circulating library in Alton and brought them over to Chawton to read with her aunts, all sharing the amusement. Isabel writes of her mother: 'In her Aunt Jane, who was the object of her most enthusiastic admiration, she found a sympathy and a companionship which was the delight of her girlhood.' I believe that Jane's portrait of Emma Woodhouse, 'handsome, clever' but possessing 'the power of having rather too much her own way, and a disposition to think a little too well of herself' probably owes something to Anna. Jane was fond of Anna as she was of her Emma, a heroine she believed 'no-one would like but herself'.

Anna has another claim to our notice. When Jane criticised the novels Anna was attempting to write, she revealed many of the principles which guided her own work. Her comments are invariably kind but detailed and searching: characters must talk and behave naturally and show no inconsistency, scenes that are 'prosy and nothing to the purpose' are best omitted. Anna must avoid novelists' slang like 'the vortex of dissipation' which, Jane remarks, is 'so old, that I dare say Adam met with it in the first novel he opened'. Most interestingly, she tells Anna she would be wise to write about people and places within her own experience, a rule that Jane follows so carefully herself. While she was writing *Mansfield Park* she enquired from Cassandra whether Northamptonshire had hedgerows like those at Steventon. Evidently Cassandra thought not, as no hedgerow scene occurs in that novel. The result of such care, even in small details, is that everything she writes convinces with its truthfulness. Jane comments on her attention to detail in a letter to her nephew Edward, also attempting a novel. She refers to 'the little bit (two inches wide) of ivory in which I work with so fine a brush, as produced little effect after much labour'. Henry tells us that although Jane wrote swiftly she subjected her work to hours of careful revision.

Our walk now becomes very beautiful as we follow the path winding in and out of the wood. Some fine beech trees remain from the woods Jane knew. The woods close around the top of the valley, and we follow their fringe to curve right towards the village of Beech. Below the woods on the opposite side of the valley our path divides. Follow the footpath sign which points straight on up the hill. Continue, keeping a fence close on your right, to climb out of the woods, walk beside a green and follow the path as it plunges steeply downhill. We are now in Beech, but the village seems so lost among the trees that only the occasional slope of a rooftop or blaze of colour from a hillside garden is visible. Cross the lane in the valley then follow the bridleway sign opposite. Our path climbs steeply to cross a green to a lane. Turn left and follow this lane through the village for a short distance until you come to a bridleway sign pointing right for Theddon.

Turn right along the path for Theddon. Pass a footpath sign on the left. When the path divides, keep straight on with the hedge on your left along a good path beside a field. You are high on the downs now and wide views over the rolling countryside open all round. Go past a bridleway sign and turn left along the lane ahead, passing Theddon Manor on your right. The lane bears left and we follow it over the downs for little over a mile. Just past the hamlet of Wivelrod look through gaps in the hedge on your left for some splendid views of Alton Abbey standing high on the opposite hillside. The large grey building is constructed to the traditional plan with a large gatehouse before the church and the cloisters beside it.

Our lane meets Abbey Road. Turn right and walk in the direction of Medstead for about two hundred yards. Look for some bungalows on the left. Immediately before the bungalows, a bridleway leads left from the road. Follow this path beside a field as it leads you gently downhill into Chawton Park wood. This wood was a favourite haunt with Jane and Cassandra and today, although the great beeches they walked beneath have gone, it is still very lovely. Slender beech saplings surround you as you enter the wood. After a few yards the path divides. Take the right hand fork. The young beeches give way to pine woods, edged with larches which trail their graceful branches over the path like long lace-trimmed sleeves. When you come to a crossways turn left to follow a beautiful woodland path almost all the way back to Chawton. You leave Chawton Park wood to follow a most delightful path running beside a meadow down a valley. On your left runs a gloriously tall and tangled hedgerow – the old-fashioned sort where blackberries, wild roses, honeysuckle and clematis wreathe themselves over hazels and hawthorns and above them rise elders, wild plums and crab apples. It was rich with fruit and Jane – whose charges included responsibility for their home-made wines – must have gathered berries on sunny afternoons.

Jane brought her visitors this way. One June afternoon in 1811, Henry called at the cottage with his London friend and business partner, Mr Tilson. Jane writes to Cassandra that after a neck of mutton for dinner, ' we all three walked to Chawton Park, meaning to go beyond it, but it was too dirty, and we were obliged to keep on the outside. Mr Tilson admired the trees very much, but grieved that they should not be turned into money.'

The footpath becomes a lane just before Chawton Park Farm. Follow the lane past the farm to join a minor road. Turn right, go under the railway bridge and walk to the traffic island on the A31. Cross the main road and follow the signs for Chawton village. Walk through the village to the corner where Jane's home stands. The oak tree, said to have been planted by Jane, became badly infected by a fungal disease and was felled in 1986. But Jean Bowden, a former curator, replanted a self-sown seedling from it on the west lawn the same year. Chawton Parish Council planted a tree in 1967 to commemorate the 150th anniversary of her death. It is the little pink-flowered chestnut tree you see on the right opposite the cottage. Jane would approve of that little tree. Her many references to trees and woods, particularly in her letters, show how much she enjoyed the woodland ways around Chawton, still so lovely today.

Above: The small chestnut tree opposite Chawton Cottage planted by the Parish Council in 1967 to commemorate the 150th anniversary of Jane's death

Right: The garden at Chawton Cottage. In the background is the oak tree, now felled, Jane is believed to have planted

Map 12

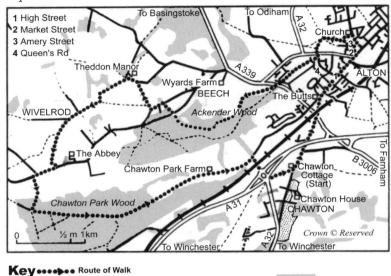

Key ••••▶•• Route of Walk

▬▬▬▬ Major Roads	– – – – Footpaths and bridleways	Woodland
▬▬▬▬ Minor Roads	+——+ Railways	Parkland

*Park in Chawton. With cottage on left follow old road through village,
under subway, over B3006 to Alton High Street. Turn left up Market Street,
right down Amery Street, church on right. Return to Amery Street, follow
footpath left of Amery Farm Veterinary Group building, round hillside to
Basingstoke Road. Turn left for a few yards then right up Ackender Road.
First right into Queen's Road. Follow footpath ahead to B3006. Cross and
follow footpath on the right, round Ackender wood. Path divides at foot of
opposite hillside. Follow footpath sign straight on to Beech. Cross lane in
valley and follow bridleway sign opposite 'To Theddon'. At lane, turn left
until you come to a bridleway sign right for Theddon. Turn right, path
divides, keep straight on through gate to lane. Follow the lane left for a
mile. When the lane meets Abbey Road, turn right for about two hundred
yards. Just before bungalows on left, turn left along footpath into Chawton
Park wood. When path divides bear right to crossways, turn left and follow
woodland path. Keep straight on out of the wood down valley path past
Chawton Park farm to minor road. Turn right, under railway, to A31.
Follow sign for Chawton.
Distance: about nine miles. Easy walking but some short steep climbs.*

13

Great Bookham and an 'Exploring Party' to Box Hill

Jane had just finished *Emma* when the Prince Regent's librarian suggested she should concern herself with a more lofty theme, perhaps write a historical romance. Jane replied politely that her interests lay in 'pictures of domestic life in country villages'. And in *Emma* she creates one of the most delightful of all 'literary' villages. 'Highbury, that airy, cheerful, happy-looking Highbury' is drawn so surely that we feel we are residents also, taking a personal interest in all that happens and acquainted with all its varied inhabitants. After sharing Harriet's agonies when snubbed by Mr Elton on the dance floor, puzzling over the infuriatingly enigmatic Jane Fairfax and marvelling at Emma's patience with the ceaseless demands of her invalid father, we can feel as Emma does that to stand in the doorway of Ford's shop in the main street of Highbury will prove interesting enough. The liveliest objects Emma could hope to see were 'Mr Perry walking hastily by; Mr William Cox letting himself in at the office door; Mr Cole's carriage horses returning from exercise; or a stray letter-boy on an obstinate mule' but 'when her eyes fell only on the butcher with his tray; a tidy old woman travelling homewards from shop with her full basket, two curs quarrelling over a dirty bone, and a string of dawdling children round the baker's little bow window eyeing the gingerbread . . . she knew she had no reason to complain'. And neither have we. No world-shaking events occur in Highbury, but after our stay there we can only agree with Sir Walter Scott that Jane's greatest gift was her 'exquisite touch, which renders ordinary commonplace things and characters interesting, from the truth of the description and the sentiment'.

Jane sets Highbury in Surrey. So real is the village that it comes as a surprise not to find it on the map. But, as R W Chapman says, there is no large village corresponding to the exact position of Highbury, sixteen miles from London, nine from Richmond and seven from Box Hill. But as Jane knew the area around Great Bookham, Leatherhead and Dorking well, it is safe to assume she had this very lovely part of Surrey in mind as the setting for the novel.

Mrs Austen's cousin, Cassandra, had married the Reverend Samuel Cooke, who was rector of Great Bookham from 1769 to 1820. The families remained close friends and Samuel Cooke was Jane's godfather. Jane spent holidays at the vicarage in Great Bookham and called there on some of her visits to Kent and London. The setting of her unfinished novel, *The Watsons*, 'in the town of D (Dorking) in Surrey' — a novel she probably began in Bath in 1804 — suggests she visited the Cookes, as she hoped to do, in 1799. After leaving Southampton, the Austens planned to stay for a while with the Cookes before travelling to Chawton. But the most interesting visit Jane paid to Great Bookham was in June 1814. She had begun writing *Emma* early in the January of the same year. Perhaps it was during this stay that she decided to set one of the most important scenes in the novel, the disastrous picnic when Emma is unkind to Miss Bates, on nearby Box Hill. This well-known beauty spot was a great attraction then as now and Jane must have joined an 'exploring party' (to quote Mrs Elton) to admire its tree-shaded cliffs and stand, as does her Emma, on the open hillside above Dorking 'in tranquil observation of the beautiful views beneath her'.

This walk follows the route of an 'exploring party', from Great Bookham to the top of Box Hill, to return along a remote wooded valley and over Fetcham Downs. The distance round is about nine miles. Apart from the short climb up Box Hill to be rewarded with wonderful views, it is easy, pleasant walking through some of the most lovely country-side in England. As you take the white paths over the Downs I am sure you will agree with Emma that 'Surrey is full of beauties'.

Great Bookham lies beside the A246, about two-and-a-half miles south-west of Leatherhead. Park in the village. Our walk begins at the church of St Nicholas, close to the cross-roads at the heart of the village in Jane's time. This small, compact church where Mrs Austen's cousin married Samuel Cooke dates back to the twelfth century. Today we can walk as they did down the nave whose round arches are supported by solid Norman pillars. But they would not see what is now the glory of this tiny church, the beautiful East window filled with six panels of fifteenth-century Flemish stained glass. The colouring is exquisite; soft, muted shades of grey and mauve contrast with a rich, glowing crimson. Leave the church by the south porch and cross the churchyard to the old coaching road which runs beside it. On your right, Church Street heads north past the present vicarage, lined with shops and cottages with the kind of old-fashioned gardens that overflow into the street. The old vicarage where Jane stayed has gone but it is said that the cedar tree you see through a gap in the row of shops opposite the church marks the site. Jane collected the opinions of her friends and relatives on her novels and the Cookes were among those for whom *Mansfield Park* made amends for her treatment of the clergy in earlier novels. (The vicar of Godmersham was particularly annoyed!) Jane writes to Cassandra: 'Mr Cooke says it is the most sensible novel he ever read and the manner in which I treat the clergy delights them very much.'

Mrs Cooke seems to have had much in common with Mrs Austen, plagued as she was with a host of minor illnesses

Overleaf: The view from Box Hill, Surrey

vaguely attributed to nerves. Jane writes: 'I told Mrs Cooke of my mother's late oppression in *her head*. She says on that subject — "Dear Mrs Austen's is I believe an attack frequent at her age and mine. Last year I had for some time the sensation of a peck loaf resting on my head." ' Perhaps Jane had Mrs Cooke in mind when she describes the extraordinary afflictions of the Parker family in *Sanditon*. Like the seekers of better health in *Sanditon*, Mrs Cooke and her daughter Mary try a month at Brighton and feel a great deal better for the sea air.

Jane found Mary Cooke a pleasant companion and compliments her beauty in the notes she added to her burlesque, 'Plan of a novel according to hints from various quarters' written after the Prince Regent's librarian had suggested she should record the history of a clergyman based on his own life. In the Plan Jane has a great deal of fun at the expense of high-flown sentiments, saintly heroes and heroines, and melodramatic events. In the margin, opposite the heroine, she notes that her eyes and cheeks are similar to those of Mary.

Opposite the church stands the Old Crown Inn which reminds us of the Crown in Highbury. But so much of the Great Bookham Jane knew has vanished beneath the tide of modern building that we cannot be certain if she took other features from the village for her Highbury. But as we start our walk we pass a row of neat eighteenth-century cottages. Turn left from the church gate and with the Old Crown Inn on your right, walk to the first turning on your right, East Street. Turn right and walk past the delightful row of cottages. The novelist Fanny Burney lived at the corner of East Street at The Hermitage after her marriage to the French émigré, General D'Arblay. Here she wrote *Camilla*, the novel which won Jane's admiration. It is interesting to speculate whether Jane ever met Fanny Burney. It seems unlikely as Jane declined an invitation to meet Madame de Stael, valuing her obscurity, but so warm was Jane's admiration that she must have liked to see the places connected with her. Opposite Number 10, turn left down a footpath which runs between high hedges to Camilla Close. Cross over and walk up to the top of Pine Dean to meet a minor road. Turn right and walk to the main road, the A246. Cross straight over and follow the road ahead, Crabtree Lane. When this bears left to Downs View Road, keep straight on along a footpath. Go straight over the crossways to follow a wide path which leaves the village behind to ascend the downs. (Ignore all side paths.) The path rises to the crest of a shallow valley. On the other side thickly-wooded slopes rise behind a snug farmstead. Keep straight ahead into the valley then right as it climbs to the top of the downs again beside a beech wood. Already, on your left you will see the steep dark outline of Box Hill contrasting with the softer slopes of the meadows on your right as they fall away into a valley. The path dips towards Crabtree Cottages, then plunges more steeply downhill, bearing left towards West Humble. If you look right now you will see the steeple of Ranmore church rising dramatically like a pointing finger above the wooded hillsides. More rounded valleys fold gently into one another as far as

Print: View from Box Hill looking towards Norbury

the horizon with the little town of Dorking nestling in the foreground. In *The Watsons* Jane tells how Elizabeth drives her newly-arrived sister Emma to the ball in Dorking. As they get closer Elizabeth remarks: 'The next turning will bring us to the turnpike. You may see the church tower over the hedge, and the White Hart is close by.' Jane probably had the Red Lion Inn opposite the church in Dorking in mind as her White Hart, the setting of Emma's ball and the scene of her kindness to Mrs Blake's small son.

Our lane drops steeply down into the valley of the River Mole. Pass the half-timbered chapel at West Humble, turn left and cross the railway. (There is Box Hill station here, so if you wish you could start and finish this walk at this point.) Walk to the main road, the A24. Turn left under the subway, then left again to cross the river by Burford Bridge. Just past the hotel you will see a white path on the right, climbing steeply up the hillside. Follow this as it takes you quickly to the top of the steepest part of the famous wooded cliff. If you would prefer a gentler climb, follow the road past the hotel a little further until you come to a minor road on the right. A footpath sign in the angle of the two roads points over the down, and an easier climb soon brings you to meet the steeper path at the top. Follow the path as it winds through the box trees and dark groves of yew and juniper along the crest of the cliff. On your left smooth turf dips to a quiet valley, but on your right the ground falls dramatically beneath massive roots of oaks and beeches. Walk in Keats' words 'through the dark pillars of those sylvan aisles' past the stone marking the spot where Major Peter Labelliere was buried. Just past the stone our path bears left to meet the minor road which zig-zags to the top of Box Hill. Turn right and follow the little path running through the trees beside the road until it brings you into the open high on the hillside above Dorking. This is a wonderful viewpoint – all southern England seems to be spread at your feet! If you walk down to the semicircular stone viewing platform, various outstanding features of the scene before you are indicated. The platform is a memorial to Leopold Salomons of Norbury Park who gave Box Hill to the nation in 1914.

The soft turf of this hillside is a likely place for the 'exploring party' from Highbury to settle and open their hampers, the carriages and horses of the gentlemen waiting above beside the road. Owing to the unthinking good humour of Mr Weston, conflicting personalities are brought into close contact and the result is misery all round! Frank Churchill, wounded by Jane Fairfax's silence, flirts with Emma to the disgust of Mrs Elton. Emma, bored, restless and irritated by her companions, for once forgets her duty to Miss Bates and comments cuttingly on her dullness. Shocked, Mr Knightley reproves her, and Emma goes home in tears. From this moment on Box Hill, Emma comes to realise her power to destroy the happiness of others. The pain one person can cause another either deliberately like Mr Elton's treatment of Harriet, or quite unthinkingly like the effect of Miss Bates' ceaseless chatter on her sensitive niece, is illustrated throughout the novel. Human happiness is destroyed as wind and rain can temporarily destroy a summer garden. And in Jane Austen's novels the result is only temporary. Harriet marries a much better man than Mr Elton, Emma realises the results of her self-delusion, repents – and the sun shines once more. Thoughtful and moving as the novel is at times, *Emma* is a happy and amusing book. Some of the most delightful moments occur when we are in the company of characters who, in real life, would prove most difficult to bear with like Miss Bates, Harriet and Mr Woodhouse.

Follow the road along the edge of Box Hill until you can see a group of houses ahead. Our way lies along the path you will see leading left just before the houses by the Box Hill village sign. Turn left along this woodland way following the bridleway sign and walk through the trees for about 200 yards to a crosstrack. Go straight over and after a few yards take the right fork (unsigned at the time of writing) to follow the bridleway as it dips downhill to the valley floor. Now a wide green way leads you through hanging woods of pines and silver birches which give way occasionally to open hillsides where groves of yews cast dark shadows over the shrubs wreathed in clematis. The valley widens as the green way brings you to meet a minor road. Turn left and follow this lane to the larger road which runs north to Mickleham. On the left you see a large red brick house with some magnificent cedars in the

Juniper Hall

garden. This is Juniper Hall, now a field centre run by the National Trust, but once the refuge of French aristocrats escaping from the revolution. Amongst others, it sheltered Madame de Stael and Talleyrand and it was here that Fanny Burney, during a visit to her sister at Mickleham, met her future husband. Turn right along the sunken footpath on the other side of the road to walk to Mickleham.

Turn right just past the church where Fanny Burney was married and walk along the side of the graveyard until you come to a footpath leading left. Follow this to the main road, the A24. Go straight over the road bearing a little left to cross the River Mole by an iron railed footbridge. A few yards further you come to a footpath on the left marked Bridleway. Follow this path (river on your left) to the point where it divides. Bear right uphill with the wood on your left. The path now runs beside a lane. When the lane bends right, continue uphill to enter the wood. Pass a track on the left and follow the path ahead round the edge of Norbury Park, keeping the fence on the left, to meet a lane. Bear left past Norbury House. When the lane turns left, keep straight on through the wood for about two hundred yards to a bridleway sign on the right. Turn right as the sign directs. When the path divides bear left keeping all the trees close on your right. Keep ahead to walk through woods downhill into a valley. Go straight over the crosstrack and follow the little path up the hillside opposite. This quickly brings you over the hill and down to the half-timbered farmstead we saw across the fields at the beginning of our walk. Bear left for a few yards then turn right and walk past the front of the farm and walk up beside a field to the track leading into Downs Way. When you come to the main road, turn left for a few yards then right down Eastwick Road. You are now back on the route we followed earlier. Turn left into Pine Dean and follow the footpath back to East Street and Great Bookham Chuch.

Map 13

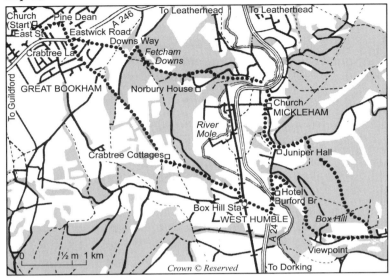

Key ••••►•• Route of Walk

▬▬▬ Major Roads	– – – – Footpaths and bridleways
▬▬▬ Minor Roads	◄—— Railways

Woodland

Parkland

*Park in Great Bookham. With the church on your left and the Crown Inn
on your right walk to the corner of East Street. Turn right up East Street,
then left along footpath to Camilla Close. Keep straight on up Pine Dean to
minor road. Turn right to A246. Cross over and follow road ahead,
Crabtree Lane. This bears left to Downs View Road, keep straight on down
footpath. Go straight over crosstrack and follow path down a valley, then
bearing right over the Downs to pass Crabtree Cottage. Turn left to valley of
the Mole. Turn left, cross the railway, to A24. Turn left over Burford Bridge
and just past Burford Bridge Hotel turn right up steep footpath to top of
Box Hill. (Gentler climb if you keep along road past the hotel a little further
to meet minor road on right. Follow direction of footpath sign in angle of
two roads, up the hill to meet steep footpath almost at the top). Follow path
along crest of hill to bear left to meet minor road by a cafe. Turn right here
and follow hillside round to viewpoint. Follow road until you see houses
ahead. Take footpath left just before houses. Go straight over crosstrack,
then right fork down into valley. Follow green way to minor road. Turn
left along road to meet the road running north to Mickleham. Turn
right for Mickleham, just past church turn right along edge of*

*graveyard then left to follow footpath to A 24. Cross Road and go over Mole by
footbridge. Follow footpath left. When path divides, bear right to walk beside a lane.
Lane bends right, follow path straight on into wood. Pass track on left and walk
around edge of Norbury Park fence on left, to lane. Bear left past Norbury Park. When
lane bears left keep straight on into wood. After about two hundred yards turn right
following bridleway sign, bear left when path divides into a valley. Go over
crosstrack up hillside ahead and down the other side to farm. Bear left for a few yards
then turn right past the front of the farm to walk up to Downs Way. At main road,
turn left, then right down Eastwick Road. Turn left into Pine Dean and follow
footpath back to East Street and Great Bookham church.*

Distance: about nine miles. Easy walking apart from short ascent of Box Hill.

14

Jane in London

Jane knew London well. She probably made her first visits on her way to stay with Edward in Kent. In her early works she adopts an almost playful approach to the great city, taking an impish delight in teasing those who saw London solely as a place of moral depravity. In *Catharine*, an unfinished novel which Jane began when she was sixteen, she makes fun of strait-laced Mrs Percival for whom London is a 'hot house of vice'. But she was not blind to the dangers that lurked in the teeming streets of Georgian London. She was fully aware that while some of the city's inhabitants lived comfortably in elegant surroundings, the majority competed for the means to live in conditions of appalling squalor. The vivid picture she draws in *Sense and Sensibility* of the fate of Colonel Brandon's childhood friend Eliza, left destitute and friendless in London, shows that she has no illusions. In a short time, through her privations, Eliza is changed from a 'lovely, blooming, healthful girl' to a 'melancholy and sickly figure' who Colonel Brandon discovers dying from consumption in a spunging house, a prison for debtors. Jane herself is wary about staying in London unless she can make definite plans to visit friends. Private philanthropy was at work in London as it was in the countryside, founding hospitals and opening charity schools, but only a fraction of its dense population could be reached by these means. In such a society, the need to make money, as Jane saw so clearly, took precedence over every other consideration. But clear-eyed as she was, Jane's view of London was a balanced one. With her delight in people she enjoyed the variety of its society, the excitement of its busy streets and shops, and the pleasures of its theatres, concerts and galleries.

The first letter Jane writes from London is dated August 1796 and headed Cork Street. Aged twenty, she is on her way to Kent, accompanied by Edward and Frank. 'Already,' she jokes to Cassandra, 'I begin to find my morals corrupted!' Her brothers have 'gone out to seek their fortunes'. In the evening they plan to go to Astleys, the large amphitheatre for equestrian performances newly opened in Westminster Bridge Road. She concludes an unusually short letter hurriedly as she is about to go out, evidently eager to see as much as possible during her short stay. Our walk of about five miles around London in Jane's footsteps starts in Piccadilly, close to Cork Street.

Constance Hill tells us that the coaches from the south and west set their passengers down in Piccadilly at The White Horse Cellar close to the entrance to the Burlington Arcade. We will imagine we have alighted with the Austen party. The White Horse Cellar is no longer visible, but just past the Arcade is Burlington House, the last of the great eighteenth-century mansions of Piccadilly that Jane would have known, though she might have some difficulty today recognising the original building behind its Victorian façade. Today it houses many august societies including the Royal Academy of Fine Arts. Jane once joked to Cassandra that now she is becoming known she will find her portrait in the Academy 'all white and red with my head on one side'. How good it would be if we had such a portrait! Our only authentic contemporary picture of Jane remains the rather disappointing pencil sketch Cassandra made of her sister now displayed in the National Portrait Gallery.

From Piccadilly, turn right into Old Bond Street. It was in this part of Mayfair that Jane set most of the London scenes in *Sense and Sensibility*. Some remaining eighteenth-century

houses with their ordered rows of windows, pillared doorways and graceful wrought-iron work remind us of the
elegant surroundings of her characters. It was from lodgings
in Bond Street that the rakish Willoughby wrote his heartless
letter to Marianne. Turn right into Burlington Gardens and
over the road on the left you will see Cork Street. Today
the old Bristol Inn, where, Constance Hill believes, Jane may
have lodged, has gone, but a few yards down the road on the
left you come to the arched approach to a narrow mews
passage. This may have been an entrance to the stables at
the back of a coaching inn. A short distance away, the name
'Coach and Horses Yard' suggests the use of this part of
Mayfair by travellers and today there is still a saddler's shop
nearby.

Leave Cork Street to turn right into Clifford Street.
Across the road you will see a fine eighteenth-century house,
built of dark red brick, its doorway flanked by Ionic columns
supporting a pediment. We can imagine the Middletons in
Sense and Sensibility in a similar house in nearby Conduit
Street. Turn right into Savile Row. On the left stands a house
Jane must have looked at with interest, the home of Richard
Brinsley Sheridan, now Hardy Amies. Go left into Vigo
Street, then immediately right to return to Piccadilly along
Sackville Street. Here was Thomas Gray's jewellers shop
where, in *Sense and Sensibility*, Elinor and Marianne had to
wait to be served while the dandy Robert Ferrars dithered
over his choice of a toothpick case.

Considering all the fascinations of London life, it is not
surprising that Jane's lively brother Henry should make his
home here. After his marriage to Eliza they lived for a while
in Sloane Street where Jane visited them. (We call there later
in our walk.) When Eliza died in 1813, Henry moved into the
city to live over the bank in which he was a partner, in Henrietta Street, near Covent Garden, in the heart of London's
theatreland. Jane came to see him soon after his removal. We
will follow her. Turn left into Piccadilly and walk round the
Circus to Coventry Street. Keep straight on past Leicester

The entrance to Goodwin's Court

Goodwin's Court

Square to the top of Cranbourne Street. 'The shops here,' Jane writes to Cassandra, 'are full of very pretty hats.' Turn right into Bear Street to meet Charing Cross Road. Cross straight over and walk down St Martin's Court to St Martin's Lane. Look over the road and a little to the right you will see a small arched entrance — just the width of a sedan chair — leading into Goodwin's Court. Cross the road, go through the arch, along a narrow passage to emerge into Jane Austen's London. The gracefully rounded bows of terraces of eighteenth-century houses face each other across a tiny walkway. It is all perfect from the carriage lamps and shining brass fittings on the doors to the carefully clipped bay trees lining the street. Leave the court by another narrow passage into Bedfordbury. Turn right for a few yards, then left down Bedford Court to Bedford Street. Over the road is Henrietta Street. Walk down the street and on the right, facing St Paul's church and still basically unaltered, is Number 10, the small town house where Jane stayed. The ground floor has been altered and the front stuccoed, but you will recognise the typically eighteenth-century neat lines of windows beneath a row of small balusters running the length of the roof. From the *London Review* Vol. 36 I discovered that inside, the front room retains its original panelling and box cornice, the staircase remains within its panelled compartment and that a back room retains its Adam-inspired chimney piece.

When Jane arrived here she sat down in 'the breakfast, dining, sitting room' to write to Cassandra. Henry's French cook, Mme Bigeon, had prepared them a 'most comfortable dinner of soup, fish, bouillée, partridges, and an apple tart'. After dinner they had gone to the Lyceum Theatre where they had a box on the stage to see *Don Juan*. Tomorrow, before breakfast, she tells Cassandra, she plans to go shopping with Fanny (Edward and some of his children are stopping for a while in town on their way to Godmersham) to buy dress lengths at Layton and Shears. Fashions are becoming more natural: 'I learnt from Mrs Tickars young lady, to my high amusement, that the stays are not made to force the bosom up.' In subsequent letters Jane tells Cassandra about accompanying Edward's children on very painful visits to the dentist. In return Jane asks her sister for their friends' opinions on *Pride and Prejudice*, recently published. Jane recorded these opinions. Although she never sought fame, concealing the secret of her authorship as long as she could, her writing was very important to her. She called *Pride and Prejudice* 'her own darling child'. She was pleased when people she valued liked her characters which were so real to her. Like most authors she worried about maintaining her standard, whether or not she might 'write herself out' and the possibility of another writer producing a clever novel that would forestall her own. But, as always with Jane, good sense ruled her personal feelings. After Henry, in an outburst of brotherly pride, had revealed her authorship, she wrote that much as she regretted this 'what a trifle it is in all its bearings, to the really important points of one's existence even in this world'.

In March 1814 Henry drove Jane from Chawton to stay in Henrietta Street again. On the way he began reading the manuscript of *Mansfield Park* and Jane reports that although he found it different from her other novels, he considered it 'by no means inferior'. He particularly liked her portrayal of Henry Crawford. Henry Crawford and his sister Mary reflect Jane's more mature feelings about London society. Both are endowed by nature with charming personalities and possess many good qualities. Unfortunately they have been brought up in contact with all that was most corrupt in London society; they are worldly, immoral and self-seeking. In *Mansfield Park* the Crawfords are contrasted strongly with the less superficially attractive Fanny Price. Although, at the end of the novel, Fanny is vindicated and the sterner moral code of the countryside prevails, the Crawfords are among the most lively and attractive of all Jane's characters. Jane enjoyed herself in London and visited Drury Lane to see Kean in the part of Shylock. His acting was perfect she told Cassandra.

Above: Henry Austen's house in Henrietta Street, Covent Garden, now the home of Acorn Computer

Interiors. Right above: Adam-inspired chimney piece

Right: Views of the staircase within its panelled compartment

From Henrietta Street, turn right into Southampton Street, then right again down the Strand. When you reach Trafalgar Square, bear left through Spring Gardens and under Admiralty Arch into the Mall. Jane records visiting an exhibition held by the Society of Painters in oil and water colours in Spring Gardens. She found a portrait exactly like Jane Bingley in *Pride and Prejudice* but alas, no one the least like Elizabeth. As you walk down the Mall you pass the white columns and arcades of Carlton Terrace on your right. Although these fine buildings were designed by Nash, shortly after Jane's death, they stand on the site of Carlton House, the Prince Regent's London home, which has special associations with her. In November 1815, James Stanier Clarke, who was the Prince Regent's librarian, wrote to Jane to say how much the Prince enjoyed her books and to invite her to visit Carlton House. While he was showing Jane over the building with its magnificent library, he told her that she had the Prince's permission to dedicate her next book, *Emma*, just about to be published, to him. With somewhat mixed feelings, we suspect, Jane asked Murrays to insert the dedication and to send a specially bound set of copies to the Prince. Mr Clarke had ideas of his own about literature. He urged Jane to write more seriously, suggesting an epic on the history of the House of Coburg or even his own life story! Jane firmly, but politely, replied she was incapable of such work. 'If it were indispensable for me to keep it up and never relax into laughing at myself or other people, I am sure I should be hung before I had finished the first chapter. No, I must keep to my own style and go on in my own way; and although I may never succeed again in that, I am convinced that I should totally fail in any other.'

Walk along the Mall, past the old palace of St James (where, in *Pride and Prejudice*, Sir William Lucas so frequently recalls his presentation) to Buckingham Palace. In Jane's time this was the Queen's house. Bear right and walk under the shade of the trees in Green Park up Constitution Hill to Hyde Park Corner. We are heading for Sloane Street where Jane first stayed with Henry and Eliza in 1811. Jane saw the parks much as we do today, but after Hyde Park Corner the scene was entirely different. The West End, as Miss Mitford tells us, was 'bordered by Hyde Park Corner on the one side and the Green Park on the other.' Sloane Street was an isolated development across an area of rather marshy ground. So Jane talks of 'walking into town' to do her shopping. Occasionally she rode in the family coach, but unlike her Mrs Elton she felt 'I had naturally small right to be parading about London in a barouche'.

Walk down Knightsbridge to turn left into Sloane Street. Jane stayed with Henry at Number 64 which has been rebuilt in Victorian Gothic style. But it is pleasant to imagine Jane here, busy correcting the proofs of *Sense and Sensibility*. One evening Eliza held a grand party with musicians and singers, inviting many of her French émigré friends. Jane enjoyed watching the company from the comparative seclusion of the hall where she chatted with George and Mary Cooke. After Eliza's death in April 1813, Henry came almost immediately to Chawton and drove Jane back with him in May to Sloane Street in his curricle. The drive, over the Hogs Back through the lovely Surrey countryside in this light, very fast carriage — the equivalent of today's sleekest sports car — gave Jane all the pleasure she attributes to Catherine Morland being driven to Northanger Abbey by Henry Tilney.

Turn right before Number 64 Sloane Street to walk down Hans Street to Hans Place, in Jane's time almost completely surrounded by fields. After his stay in Henrietta Street, Henry came to live at Number 23. Turn left, and walk a few yards round Hans Place to the house which, although rebuilt, has a plaque recalling Jane's visits to Henry here. If you walk a little further to look at Number 30, you will see the most charming eighteenth-century house with rounded windows and a delicate wrought-iron balcony. Henry's house must have been as attractive, because Jane thought it 'a delightful place'. She saw it for the first time in August 1814. Later in the year, in November, she came again, to see *Emma* safely through the press. Henry had worked hard on her behalf. When Egerton refused to re-issue *Mansfield Park* he arranged with Murrays of Albermarle Street for a second edition and they also agreed to publish *Emma*. Jane was very busy preparing *Mansfield Park* for its second edition, correcting the proofs of *Emma* and when she could, continuing her new novel *Persuasion*. In the middle of all this, Henry fell seriously ill and Jane nursed him devotedly. It was no wonder that her own health began to fail. But by December Henry was better and *Emma* safely published and Jane could return to Chawton. Soon after, Henry's business failed and he decided to take Holy Orders and live near Chawton. So the elegant little house in Hans Place was given up.

We end our London walk in Hans Place. Enough remains of Jane's London to help us to recapture the atmosphere of the London scenes in her novels. Although she is more often considered as a painter of 'domestic life in country villages', I believe that Jane's experience of the city enriches her work and gives depth and contrast to her characters. Her sympathies may lie with the countryside, but who could part with Henry and Mary Crawford, reflecting, as they do, their creator's enjoyment of the variety and excitement of London life?

Map 14

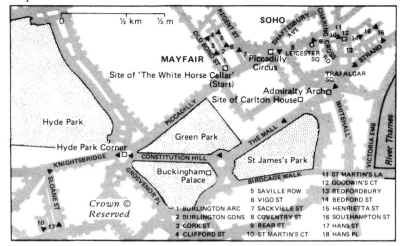

Key   ► Route of Walk

Start in Piccadilly, near entrance to Burlington Arcade. Turn right into Old Bond Street, right into Burlington Gardens, cross road to Cork Street. Right into Clifford Street, right into Savile Row. Left into Vigo Street, right down Sackville Street to Piccadilly. Left round Circus to Coventry Street, past Leicester Square to Cranbourne Street. Right down Bear Street to Charing Cross Road. Cross straight over, down St Martin's Court to St Martin's Lane. Look over road and a little to the right you will see an archway leading into eighteenth-century Goodwin's Court. Leave Court by passage to Bedfordbury. Right, then left down Bedford Court to Bedford Street. Over the road is Henrietta Street. Walk to end, turn right into Southampton Street, then right into the Strand. Walk past Trafalgar Square, under Admiralty Arch and along the Mall. Bear right round Buckingham Palace, up Constitution Hill to Hyde Park Corner. Go through underpass to Knightsbridge and walk to Sloane Street on left. Walk down Sloane Street to Number 64, turn right here down Hans Street to Hans Place. Pass Number 23 (where Jane stayed) to see remaining eighteenth-century house, Number 30. Distance: about five miles. There is so much to see that this really needs a day.

15

Winchester — Jane's last Journey

Early in 1816, when she was forty, friends noticed a difference in Jane's manner. She was more serious and when she revisited places she knew, looked at them as if it was to be the last time. As the year advanced, she suffered increasingly from fever and weakness, symptoms of Addison's disease, at that time undiagnosed and therefore impossible to treat. In May she visited Cheltenham with Cassandra, but the waters were of no benefit. But neither her courage nor her artistic sense deserted her. In July, she finished the first version of *Persuasion*, one of the most beautiful love stories ever written and the most tender and romantic of all her novels. She felt the ending was 'flat and tame' and in reviewing the last two chapters, added another containing the brilliantly written scene in the White Hart in Bath, when Captain Wentworth overhears Anne Elliot defend the constancy of woman's love. This time, Jane allows her readers to share all the conflicting emotions felt by the lovers. The letters she wrote at this time to her nephews and nieces show the same increase in tenderness, particularly those to Fanny who repeatedly seeks her advice on love. As we would expect from reading her novels and the example of her own life, Jane advises her to make quite certain of her feelings: 'Nothing can be compared to the misery of being bound without love, bound to one, and preferring another.'

After finishing *Persuasion* her illness increased, but she

remained optimistic. In January 1817 she wrote to Caroline
that she was now so well she could walk to Alton without
fatigue. It is a tribute to her courage — and her sense of
humour — that about this time she began an amusing new
novel about invalids, *Sanditon*. But in a letter to Fanny in
March there are hints she is worse. 'By sitting down and resting a good while between my walks, I get exercise enough.'
When Caroline called with her sister Anna in April, she found
her aunt Jane in her room 'sitting quite like an invalid in an
armchair'. Although obviously very weak, Jane welcomed
them kindly. The same month, her uncle Leigh Perrot died
and possibly his neglect of her mother in his will depressed
her. Jane made her will, leaving everything to Cassandra,
apart from fifty pounds to Henry and another fifty pounds

*The house in College Street, Winchester, where Jane and
Cassandra lodged*

to his housekeeper who had lost her savings when he was declared bankrupt.

Jane was being treated by Mr William Curtis, the apothecary at Alton. He called in the help of the surgeon-in-ordinary at the county hospital in Winchester, Mr Giles King Lyford, and Jane seemed to improve under his care. So it was decided Jane should travel the sixteen miles to Winchester to be treated by him. On a wet Saturday in May 1817, Jane made the journey with Cassandra in James's coach, escorted by Henry and young William Knight on horseback.

Jane and Cassandra took lodgings in Number 8, College Street. Today the house remains, unchanged, in this quiet street facing the walls and gardens of the Cathedral Close. You will see a plaque at first-floor level, commemorating Jane's stay. Jane immediately felt better. 'Our lodgings are very comfortable,' she writes cheerfully to her nephew James Edward. 'We have a neat little drawing room with a bow-window overlooking Dr Gabell's garden.' Today we can stand beneath the bow, and imagine Jane there, looking over the walls to the towers of the great cathedral which she admired very much. But in spite of her light-hearted letters, an outing in a sedan chair and plans to be promoted to a wheel chair in the summer, there was little Dr Lyford could do for her. In the early hours of Friday, 18 July, Jane died peacefully in Cassandra's arms. She was just forty-one. The following Thursday she was borne on her last journey to be buried in the cathedral. She was accompanied by her brothers, Edward, Henry and Frank, and her nephew James Edward, in the place of his father who was ill. At that time, ladies did not often attend funerals, but Cassandra revealed her grief in letters to Fanny. 'I watched the little procession the length of the street,' she writes. 'Never was human being more sincerely mourned by those who attended her remains than was this dear creature.'

If you follow Jane's last journey, over the peaceful lawns of the Cathedral Close, you will find the surroundings still as lovely today as they were then. From College Street, turn

Kingsgate, Winchester

right under Kingsgate, then right again through the old arch
leading into the Close. Walk towards the cloisters along the
south side of the cathedral. Enter the cathedral by the west
door. You will find the dark slab marking Jane's grave in the
north aisle of the nave. Close by, on the wall, is a brass memorial to her and above it a window erected in her memory in
1900. As I stood in the north aisle, October sunlight flooded
through the great windows of this beautiful cathedral,
bringing out the warmth of its ancient, honey-coloured
stones. A fitting resting place for one of England's happiest
writers. Throughout her work, we sense Jane's steady belief
that it is possible for human beings, however fallible, to build
an ordered, loving society. Jane Austen's novels will always
be read with delight.

The City Museum is close to the cathedral, and has a small
room dedicated to Jane Austen. Here you will find a portrait
of her, some of her comic verse, some very pretty bead purses
and an ivory spool case engraved with her initials.

Entrance to the Cathedral Close, Winchester

Book List

Jane Austen's Letters Ed. R W Chapman, OUP 1932 2nd ed. revised 1959

My Aunt Jane Austen Caroline Austen (Printed for the Jane Austen Society 1952)

A Memoir of Jane Austen J E Austen-Leigh 2nd ed. 1871

Jane Austen, Her Life and Letters W and R A Austen-Leigh, Smith Elder & Co. 1913

Jane Austen and Her World Marghanita Laski, Thames & Hudson 1975

A Jane Austen Companion F B Pinion, Macmillan 1973

Jane Austen, Her Homes and Her Friends Constance Hill, John Lane 1902

Steventon and the Austens Keith Iron (Available in Steventon Church)

Jane Austen and Steventon Rev W B Norris (Available from 2 Wonston Manor Cottages, Sutton Scotney, Winchester, 30p plus postage)

Jane Austen and Godmersham Rev S Graham Brade-Birks (Available from Maidstone and Ashford Libraries)

Jane Austen in Bath Jean Freeman (Printed for the Jane Austen Society 1969)

Jane Austen in Lyme Henry Chessell

Lyme Regis Walkabout Chapman & Clayton 1975

Jane Austen and Southampton R A Austen-Leigh

Southampton, a Biography A Temple Patterson, Macmillan 1970

The Story of Jane Austen's Chawton Home T Edward Carpenter (Published by the Jane Austen Memorial Trust)

An Account of the Commemoration of the 150th Anniversary of the Death of Jane Austen, Chawton 1967 Anne Mallinson (Available from Selborne Bookshop).

Survey of London Vol. 36 The Companion Guide to London David Piper, Collins 1974

Jane Austen in Winchester Canon F Bussby (Available in the Cathedral)

A Hampshire Treasury Margaret Green, Winton Publications 1972

The Oxford Literary Guide to the British Isles Dorothy Eagle and Hilary Carnell 1977

NOTES

NOTES